Educating Children and Young People with Acquired Brain Injury

Educating Children and Young People with Acquired Brain Injury is an authoritative resource book on the effects of brain injury on young people and how educators can understand and support their needs. This new edition has been updated to reflect changes to legislation and practice relating to special educational needs and will enable you to maximise the learning opportunities for young people with acquired brain injury (ABI). Considering key areas in special educational needs such as communication, interaction, cognition, sensory and physical needs, the book provides information on the multifaceted needs of children and young people with ABI and how these needs can be met.

This book will help you to:

- Understand the difficulties that young people with ABI experience
- Support these students by using appropriate strategies to help their learning
- Understand and address the social and emotional difficulties experienced by these students
- Work in partnership with families and other professionals
- Understand information from other professionals by reference to a glossary of terms
- Access further useful information from relevant resources and organisations

Written for SENCOs, teachers, teaching assistants, educational psychologists and other education professionals across all settings, *Educating Children and Young People with Acquired Brain Injury* is full of useful information and advice for parents and other family members, therapists and support workers involved with children and young people with ABI.

Sue Walker is an Educational Psychologist specialising in the needs of children with acquired brain injury.

Beth Wicks is an Education Consultant specialising in the needs of students with acquired brain injury.

Educating Children and Young People with Acquired Brain Injury

SECOND EDITION

Sue Walker and Beth Wicks

Routledge
Taylor & Francis Group

LONDON AND NEW YORK

Second edition published 2018
by Routledge
2 Park Square, Milton Park, Abingdon, Oxon, OX14 4RN

and by Routledge
711 Third Avenue, New York, NY 10017

Routledge is an imprint of the Taylor & Francis Group, an informa business

First edition published by David Fulton 2005

British Library Cataloguing-in-Publication Data
A catalogue record for this book is available from the British Library

Library of Congress Cataloging-in-Publication Data
Names: Walker, Sue, 1954– author. | Wicks, Beth (Education consultant), author.
Title: Educating children and young people with acquired brain injury / Sue Walker and Beth Wicks.
Description: 2nd edition. | Abingdon, Oxon ; New York, NY : Routledge, 2018. | Revised edition of: The education of children with acquired brain injury. London : David Fulton, 2003. | Includes bibliographical references.
Identifiers: LCCN 2017037576 (print) | LCCN 2017058498 (ebook) | ISBN 9781315453699 (ebook) | ISBN 9781138211018 (hbk) | ISBN 9781138211025 (pbk) | ISBN 9781315453699 (ebk)
Subjects: LCSH: Brain-damaged children—Education—Great Britain.
Classification: LCC LC4580 (ebook) | LCC LC4580 .W25 2018 (print) | DDC 371.91—dc23
LC record available at https://lccn.loc.gov/2017037576

ISBN: 978-1-138-21101-8 (hbk)
ISBN: 978-1-138-21102-5 (pbk)
ISBN: 978-1-315-45369-9 (ebk)

Typeset in Celeste
by Apex CoVantage, LLC

Contents

Acknowledgements

We would like to acknowledge Noel Gunther, the person from Brainline.com who willingly gave permission for reproduction of information from its blog.

We would like to thank all the children and their families with whom we have both worked over the years and who have taught us so much about acquired brain injuries.

Preface

There is increasing awareness of the long-term effects of acquired brain injuries (ABI) in children and young people, both in the UK and internationally. However, this is largely in the worlds of medicine and academic research, with many of those in education remaining unaware of the ways in which ABI can affect young peoples' progress and potential. This has been mainly as a result of a lack of relevant information for education professionals, and the first edition of this book was produced to meet growing demands for such information.

Since then there has been an increase in the awareness and knowledge of many education professionals, but recent research indicates that progress in this respect continues slowly. There is, therefore, still a need for this information for educators. There have also been changes to:

- Special education and disability legislation in the UK: the Special Educational Needs and Disability Code of Practice now covers the 0–25 age range, whereas the focus of the first edition was on school-aged children;
- The knowledge of those working within the brain injury field since the first edition.

This second edition includes older adolescents and young adults together with updated information and references to reflect both of these issues.

Acquired brain injury is more common than most people realise. In fact, if you are an educator, it is very likely that you will already have worked with one or more students who have this condition. You may not have been aware of this!

The aim of this book is to provide information that will enable the optimum abilities and potential of students with acquired brain injury to be realised in the education environment.

We hope the information in this book will help to broaden the awareness and understanding of issues related to the education of these students, together with practical suggestions for strategies and provisions that have been successfully used with them.

Note: Throughout this publication, we have used 'he' and 'him' to represent both sexes in order to avoid cumbersome phraseology.

Introduction

BEN'S STORY

Ben was 11 years old when he was hit by a car while out riding his bike. He was taken by ambulance to his local hospital and then transferred to the regional hospital which had more specialist facilities for managing his acquired brain injury. He was in a coma for two weeks. As he regained consciousness, he was confused and aggressive but these problems resolved. With a lot of help and therapy in hospital, Ben gradually regained his superficial physical and communication skills. He made excellent progress, and when he was discharged everyone said what a remarkable recovery he had made. Ben and his parents were very enthusiastic about his return to school and looking forward to the whole family being able to get back to normal. His friends and teachers made a fuss of him at first; they were very relieved to see he had made a 'complete recovery', and pleased to see him back at school. They thought that he just needed to catch up with the work he had missed.

But Ben has changed in a number of ways. It takes him much longer to get things done and he often doesn't finish them. He is easily distracted and has trouble remembering information, even very simple instructions. He seems to forget what his teacher tells him from one minute to the next. He can't always find the words he wants to use and reading is much harder for him than it used to be. He gets easily tired and irritable. His friends are not spending much time with him now; he can't keep up with the things they like to do and talk about, and they laugh at his silly comments and behaviour and think he is stupid. They also don't like the way he gets angry; he never used to. Ben's teachers and friends are beginning to think that he is different from the Ben they knew before the accident.

They are finding it difficult to understand all the changes that have happened to him.

What is an acquired brain injury?

Acquired brain injury (ABI) refers to any injury occurring to the brain after birth and the immediate neonatal period. The term 'acquired' describes brain injury sustained after a period of normal development. Such injuries may be caused by accidents or from diseases or infections. The term does not include brain injury that is congenital (i.e. present at or before birth), produced by birth trauma, or degenerative in nature.

Traumatic brain injury (TBI) is an acquired brain injury that is caused by external forces – accidents or other injuries – and **atraumatic** or **non-traumatic brain injury** is caused by illness or infection.

Numbers of children affected

Acquired brain injury (ABI) is a leading cause of disability in childhood (Forsyth and Kirkham 2012). It has sometimes been referred to as the 'silent epidemic' of our times.

Traumatic brain injury

The incidence of hospitalisation for traumatic brain injury (TBI) in England has been reported as ranging from 280–500 per 100,000 children aged from 1 to 16 years, implying that the total number of children admitted to hospital for TBI per annum in the UK is at least 35,000. Of these, approximately 2,000 will have sustained severe TBI, 3,000 moderate TBI and 30,000 mild TBI (NHS England 2013). Published hospital figures do not include a significant number of injuries that go unreported for a number of reasons, for instance if they have orthopaedic injuries and are recorded under these. Also, some children with less severe injuries may not be admitted to hospital. There is increasing evidence that even mild injuries can cause long-lasting effects (see Chapter 13).

Non-traumatic brain injury

Collectively, significant numbers of non-traumatic brain injuries also add to the total number of children affected, although each individual illness or injury cause is not common. The same 2013 NHS report cited above states that, per annum, approximately 4,000 children will suffer coma resulting from encephalopathy, 525 will be diagnosed with brain tumours and 200–300 will suffer a stroke.

Survival from acquired brain injury

Improved emergency response systems and medical advances have greatly increased the survival rate of children who are injured (Forsyth and Kirkham, 2012). The majority of children who suffer ABI survive the initial injury or illness and have no subsequent reduction in life expectancy. However, any effects of that injury, caused by damage to the brain, also persist so that children and adults continue to live with these consequences.

Numbers of ABI survivors within education

The enormity of the problem is a cumulative one. The most important figures to consider are not ones of **incidence** – frequency of occurrence – but **prevalence** – numbers currently affected. There are no accurate figures for this, but if one considers that at least 1 in 500 children under 16 years of age will sustain a TBI *each year* and that this number will be increased by the addition of the accumulated numbers of lower-incidence, non-traumatic injuries, it is very clear that it is not a rare condition. It has been estimated that, in terms of TBI alone, 3% of the population will be affected by the time they reach adolescence (Mira et al. 1992). Many schools and colleges, therefore, are likely to have students who have an acquired brain injury.

References

Forsyth, R. and Kirkham, F. (2012) 'Predicting outcome after childhood brain injury'. *CMAJ: Canadian Medical Association Journal* 184 (11), pp. 1257–1261.

Mira, M. P., Tucker, B. F. and Tyler, J. S. (1992) *Traumatic Brain Injury in Children and Adolescents: A Sourcebook for Teachers and Other School Personnel.* Austin, TX: Pro-Ed.

NHS England (2013) NHS Standard Contract for Paediatric Neurosciences: Neurorehabilitation Service Specification Number 1 NHS England/E09/S/ (www.england.nhs.uk/wp-content/uploads/2013/06/e09-paedi-neurorehabilitation.pdf).

Understanding the developing brain

The human brain is quite elegantly the supreme organ of learning. All that a person does, all that a person is, emanates from the brain.

(Savage 1994)

The brain controls every aspect of human life. It is responsible for everything we do and think, from basic bodily functions, such as breathing, blood pressure and sleep control, to the expression of personality and emotions, and control of thoughts and behaviour. It controls our ability to move, sense things, plan and organise, and communicate, etc. It may therefore seem surprising that few of us understand or have been taught much about the brain, as the all-important part of our body that enables us to know who we are and what we do.

It is helpful to recognise what the brain does and how it works in order to appreciate what might have happened when it is injured and therefore may not work efficiently.

The following description of the basic structure and function of the brain is presented in a simplistic, non-technical way. This is not meant to trivialise the topic, but to provide an accessible and introductory guide to readers who may not be familiar with this. More detailed information about brain development and functioning can be found in Reed and Warner-Rogers (2008).

Structure of the brain

The central nervous system is made up of the brain and the spinal cord. The spinal cord is a bundle of nerves that connects the brain to other parts of the body. It receives signals from all parts of the body, relays information upwards and downwards from the brain and is protected by a series of bones called vertebrae, collectively known as the vertebral column. Although the spinal cord is susceptible to damage, the results of a spinal cord injury are very different from those of injuries to the brain and are therefore not referred to here.

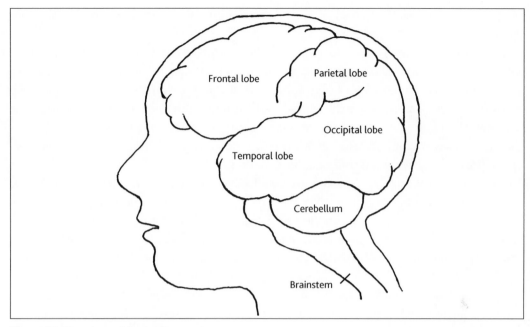

Figure 1.1 Structure of the brain

The brain is a complex structure. The terminology that has evolved to describe it is also complex and most structures have acquired several alternative labels derived from Greek, Latin, English or French.

The brain can be described as having three major parts: the brainstem, the cerebellum and the cerebral cortex. However, although each area has specific functions, they are not distinct or separate working units but an organisation of multiple and interconnected systems that are heavily dependent on each other (see Figure 1.1).

The **brainstem** is the lowest part of the brain, which tapers into the spinal cord. In lay terms it can be said to function like a telecommunications cable (Powell 1994): a collection of nerves and fibres carrying all messages backwards and forwards between the brain and the rest of the body. However, the brainstem is also responsible for basic bodily functions essential to life such as breathing, heart rate and blood pressure, and plays a vital role in basic attention, arousal and consciousness.

The **cerebellum** – meaning 'little brain' – is a cauliflower-like structure that sits under the cerebral cortex. It controls and co-ordinates bodily movement and muscle tone – the degree of muscle tension during rest or in response to stretching. It develops and stores information regarding the motor – i.e. physical – skills that enable us to walk, run, climb, ride bikes, carry out fine motor activities such as handwriting or using a knife and fork, and many other physical activities. The cerebellum helps control direction, rate, force and smoothness of movement. It is situated just above the brainstem at the back of the brain and is thus relatively well protected from traumatic injury compared with other parts of the brain.

The **cerebral cortex** is the largest part of the brain, dedicated to the highest levels of thinking, moving and acting, and makes up seven-tenths of the entire nervous system in humans. It is shaped like a large walnut: its surface is convoluted with many deep furrows – sulci – and raised surfaces – gyri – enabling increased surface area within the confines of a relatively small skull. Neuroscientists believe that it is the cerebral cortex that sets us apart from all other creatures. The outer layer of the cortex has a greyish appearance and is often referred to as 'grey matter'.

The cerebral cortex is divided into two halves: the **right and left hemispheres**. Although similar in appearance, they have different functions. The left cerebral hemisphere controls the right side of the body and is usually responsible for speech and language functions; the right cerebral hemisphere controls the left side of the body and is usually responsible for processing visual and spatial information and some other non-verbal skills.

The differences in specialities in the right and left hemispheres can indicate that an injury to the left side of the brain would be more likely to result in language difficulties and/or right-sided problems, while injury to the right side of the brain may produce difficulties with visual perception and/or left-sided problems. However, it is important to note that, although some brain injuries may only affect a specific area or areas, many lead to more widely spread damage (see Chapter 2).

The two hemispheres are linked by nerve fibres, collectively called the corpus callosum, which serve as a bridge or channel of communication between the hemispheres.

Each hemisphere is further divided into four parts, or lobes: occipital, parietal, temporal and frontal. These are named after the overlying bones of the skull. Each lobe is associated with different aspects of functioning:

- **Occipital lobes**, at the very back of the head, are involved in processing visual information. This includes visual acuity – often just termed 'vision' – and the way visual information is interpreted, e.g. colour, word or object recognition.

- **Parietal lobes** are located at the back and top of the head, behind the frontal lobes and above the temporal lobes. They are responsible for the processing of information about body sensation – touch, pressure, temperature and pain – as well as the integration of visual and auditory information and an understanding of spatial relationships.

- **Temporal lobes** are located under the temples and are important for hearing and many aspects of memory. They are crucially involved in certain processes relating to attention and language, to musical ability, and to facial and other aspects of visual recognition. An area of the brain called Wernicke's Area spans the temporal and parietal lobes and is partly responsible for our understanding and production of language. Deep within each temporal lobe is also a structure called the **hippocampus** – named thus as its shape is said to resemble a seahorse. This plays an important role in memory and is linked with other areas involved with emotion.

- **Frontal lobes** are located behind the forehead. They are relatively immature during childhood and develop over an extended period into early adulthood. They are extremely vulnerable to injury because of their location at the front of the head (McAllister 2011). The frontal lobes are responsible for some motor functions and some aspects of memory but are particularly important in respect of ability in problem solving, initiation, judgement, impulse control, etc. They act as 'behavioural regulators', planning and evaluating behavioural responses. These, along with other behaviours, are known as '**executive functions**' (see Chapter 4).

  The frontal lobes also contain a structure known as Broca's Area that is associated with our ability to speak and also, to some extent, to understand language (Caplan 2006).

There are other structures deep within the centre of the brain that have important functions, such as those relating to emotion and sleep control.

Protection of the brain

The brain is protected and nourished in a number of ways:

- **Skull or cranium**: This is the hard bone that surrounds the brain and generally serves to protect it. However, the inner surface of the skull has some bony ridges – most particularly in the frontal area – which can result in damage to the soft brain tissue if shaken against it.

- **Meninges**: The brain is covered by three layers of membrane, known collectively as the meninges. The outer one, called the **dura**, is like a very tough plastic sheet and protects the brain from movement, but not if this is excessive or violent. The two inner layers are more delicate.

- **Cerebrospinal fluid (CSF)**: CSF is a clear watery-like liquid that surrounds and cushions the brain. It circulates throughout four hollow chambers within the brain called **ventricles** and around the brain and spinal cord, acting like a shock absorber. CSF also removes brain waste products and provides the brain with nutrients. New CSF is constantly being produced while old fluid is released and absorbed into blood vessels.

- **Blood**: Blood provides oxygen and nutrients for the brain; a blood-brain barrier filters the blood and provides some, but not complete, protection to the brain from any chemicals in the blood that could be toxic.

Brain development

Growth before birth

Initially, the human embryo consists of only a few primitive cells which develop into the body and all its vital organs. Brain tissue is made up primarily of nerve cells – or **neurons** – and supporting cells called **glial** – meaning glue – cells. During a very early stage of foetal development – week three of gestation – something called the neural tube is formed, which is mainly comprised of neural stem cells and is filled with cerebrospinal fluid. Neurons – and glial cells – are produced; this is called neurogenesis. These initially form a basic front, mid- and hindbrain and then the newly formed neurons move to form other brain structures. This migration is guided partly by paths created by glial cells, which direct the neurons to their ultimate location. When they reach their destination, the cells start to specialise.

By week nine of foetal development, the brain has already taken on its adult shape, with the typical convolutions – folds – of the cortex. The growth and development of the brain in the womb is more accelerated than any other part of the foetus; a newborn baby's brain is one-third of the adult brain weight, although the baby's overall weight is one-twentieth as heavy as the adult it will become – the average weight of a brain in a newborn baby is 450 g and by adulthood the average weight is 1,400 g. As a result, when babies are born their heads are very large in relation to the rest of their body.

Neurogenesis continues during the first few months of life. It was previously thought that after this initial production of neural cells during early development, no new neurons could be generated, but we now know that limited natural neurogenesis continues in adults, in certain brain regions (Paspala et al. 2011). Currently this has been identified primarily in the hippocampus – see description of temporal lobes, pages 6–7. There is also considerable current interest and research regarding the potential use of stem cells in cell replacement therapy.

Prenatal neural development is thought to be mainly genetically determined. Interruptions to development during this period, such as trauma or infection, are likely to have a significant impact on cerebral structure.

Growth after birth

A newborn baby's brain has about a hundred billion cells, but they have only just begun to develop the connections that enable the brain to be an organised and integrated system. The nerve cells, or neurons, continue to grow, sprouting thin fibres, called **dendrites**, like wide, sprawling branches of a tree. These fibres enable cells to receive information in the form of electrical or chemical messages. Each cell also has a single thinner and potentially very long fibre called an **axon**, which transmits

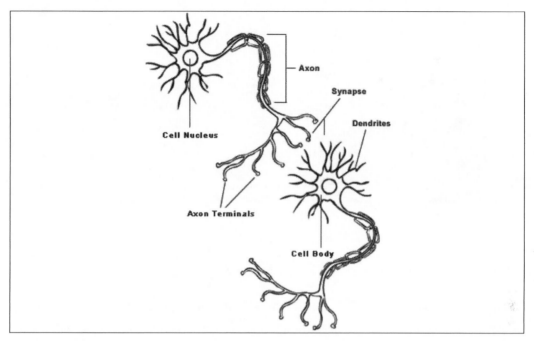

Figure 1.2 Neural network

messages. The ends of axons do not actually touch dendrites, as there are minute gaps, called **synapses**, over which these chemical or electrical messages must travel. When cells connect together in this way, they form what are known as **neural networks** (see Figure 1.2). An important substance called **myelin** is produced which gradually forms a protective sheath around the axons over time. This serves to insulate the axons and to increase the speed at which messages can be transmitted, therefore making those brain functions more efficient. There is a time of particularly rapid **myelination** during a child's early months and years.

Very complex patterns of communication develop as the brain continues to grow – involving creation of new neural networks, expansion of existing ones and continued myelination – throughout childhood. Its development is not rigidly predetermined; it gradually evolves over a lifetime. In contrast to development before birth, as postnatal development involves the process of developing and strengthening connections between neurons – and discarding ones that are no longer useful – it is more susceptible to environmental influences. Brain damage sustained postnatally usually has less impact on overall brain structure, but may interfere with this ongoing elaboration of the central nervous system and the development of interconnections and functional systems within it (Anderson et al. 2001); i.e. injury can alter normal developmental progression.

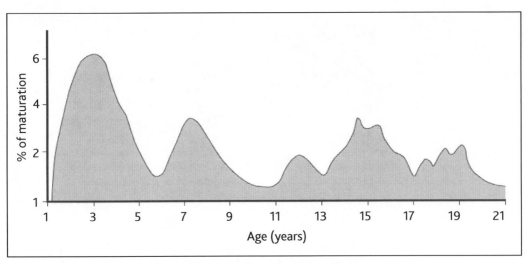

Figure 1.3 Growth of the brain after birth (adapted from Savage 1999)

The graph in Figure 1.3 illustrates the ongoing development of the brain throughout infancy, childhood and late teens/early adult years. As illustrated, five peak periods of brain growth have been identified, at approximately:

years 1–6
7–10
11–13
14–17
18–21

The brain develops in an ordered, hierarchical way, and different regions of the brain have particular growth periods which occur at different chronological ages, with the frontal regions being the last to fully mature. The 'peaks and troughs' reinforce the view that children have growth spurts, both physically and cognitively.

Although the brain's fastest rate of growth is in infancy and early childhood – it reaches about 75% of its adult weight by about the age of 3, and 90% by the age of 6 – it continues to grow and is not fully mature until early adulthood. This protracted period of maturation is unique to humans and reflects the complexity of the mechanisms and the range of developmental processes that evolve. Certain brain areas take longer than others to mature, or to come 'on-line'.

No two brains are ever exactly the same, even those of genetically identical twins.

References

Anderson, V., Northam, E., Hendy, J. and Wrennall, J. (2001) *Developmental Neuropsychology: A Clinical Approach*. Hove, East Sussex: Psychology Press.

Caplan, D. (2006) 'Why is Broca's Area involved in syntax?'. *Cortex* 42 (4), pp. 469–471.

McAllister, T. W. (2011) 'Neurobiological consequences of traumatic brain injury'. *Dialogues in Clinical Neuroscience* 13 (3), pp. 287–300.

Paspala, S. A. B., Murthy, T. V. R. K., Mahaboob, V. S. and Habeeb, M. A. (2011) 'Pluripotent stem cells: A review of the current status in neural regeneration'. *Neurology India* 59 (4), pp. 558–565.

Powell, T. (1994) *Head Injury: A Practical Guide.* Nottingham: Headway National Head Injuries Association Ltd (2nd edition published 2001, Bicester: Winslow).

Reed, J. and Warner-Rogers, J. (2008) *Child Neuropsychology: Concepts, Theory and Practice.* Chichester, UK: Wiley-Blackwell.

Savage, R. C. (1994) 'An educator's guide to the brain and brain injury', in Savage, R. C. and Wolcott, G. F. (eds) *Educational Dimensions of Acquired Brain Injury.* Austin, TX: Pro-Ed, pp. 13–31.

Savage, R. C. (1999) *The Child's Brain: Injury and Development.* Wake Forest, NC: Lash and Associates Publishing/Training Inc.

What happens in brain injury?

The nature, type, and severity of brain injury affect the outcome and long-term sequelae associated with such injury in children.

(Semrud-Clikeman 2007)

Child brain injury can be considered a chronic condition with lifelong implications.

(Reed et al. 2015)

Chapter 1 described the complex functions and development of the brain – an amazing 'computer' which exists within the solid 'box' of bone that is the skull, maintaining the person each of us is and enabling us to live and breathe. However, there are ways in which these delicate systems and functions can be disrupted, with potentially devastating effects. The mechanics and effects of an organic injury to the brain are described below.

Causes

Injury to the brain can occur as a result of a blow or force physically exerted to the body from outside, as a result of an illness or internal imbalance, or as a result of deprivation of an element essential for efficient functioning.

All injuries to the brain (after birth) are termed acquired brain injuries, an umbrella term that includes **traumatic brain injuries (TBI)** – those caused by an external force and previously sometimes referred to as 'head injuries' – and **atraumatic** or **non-traumatic brain injuries** – those caused by all other means.

External forces – traumatic injuries

Penetrating injury

These injuries occur when an object penetrates the skull and the delicate brain tissue beneath. This type of injury can occur, for instance, from some gunshot or knife wounds.

In such cases, the exact site of the injury and the damaged area of the brain may be apparent. However, injuries to the substance of the brain can be more widespread, even though the damage may initially seem localised.

Impact and deceleration injuries

More common are injuries when an object does not actually penetrate the brain itself. This often happens in, for instance, falls, sports injuries, road traffic accidents and assaults. The head may well come into contact with a hard object – e.g. the ground or part of a vehicle – which may or may not fracture the skull, but this object does not invade the tissue of the brain. This is called a **closed head injury**. Sometimes part of the skull itself is pushed inwards, which can create an **open head injury** with a depressed skull fracture. The depressed skull fragments may damage surface areas of the brain, but the penetration is by small pieces of bone, not an external object.

Sometimes there is little or no obvious damage to the outside of the head or skull, but the damage is caused by violent shaking of the brain. The inside of the skull is struck with force and the brain may rebound from back to front or side to side. This can happen in road traffic accidents, when the person is propelled forwards at speed but the body then stops abruptly. It can also result from babies or children being shaken. The protective effects of the meninges and cerebrospinal fluid may be insufficient to prevent injury. The tissue of the brain can be bruised or may bleed and the violent shaking can tear the microscopic but vital connections between neurons – the neural networks. When axons in a wider area of the brain are damaged, this is termed a **diffuse axonal injury**. When an initial site of injury – for instance, caused by a blow – is to one side of the brain, but then the brain rebounds and is injured by an additional, corresponding impact with the inside of the skull on the opposite side, this is called **contrecoup injury**.

Other injuries

Any injuries that restrict available oxygen to the brain can result in damage. For instance, youngsters who have nearly drowned in pools or ponds or who have choked may recover but may have sustained damage. Similar results may be seen from deliberate or accidental hanging or other types of asphyxiation. Cells in the brain deprived of oxygen will die.

Illness – non-traumatic injuries

Infections of the brain and surrounding tissue

Meningitis most often, but not exclusively, affects children and young adults. It can be caused by a variety of organisms but most usually by a viral or bacterial infection that causes inflammation of the outer membranes covering the brain and spinal cord: the **meninges**. Meningitis caused by bacterial infection is less common but is the most serious form of the illness and can quickly cause severe brain injury and be life threatening. Viral meningitis is usually less severe. Survivors of this illness can be left with damage to specific aspects of brain function, including deafness. Sometimes septicaemia, a serious life-threatening condition, accompanies bacterial meningitis, with a range of potential outcomes such as the loss of limbs or scarring.

Encephalitis is the result of infection that causes inflammation throughout the brain itself, not just the meninges. Many different viruses can be responsible for causing this illness, including ones commonly seen in childhood, such as measles, rubella or chicken pox. In certain rare cases, these viruses affect the brain, or provoke it to respond with an allergic reaction. Occasionally, the cause may be a bacterial or fungal agent and, even more rarely, the body's immune system appears to 'attack' parts of the brain, either following a viral infection or for no apparent reason. Some viruses that cause encephalitis are spread via insect bites, although this is very uncommon in the UK where the most common cause of encephalitis is the cold sore virus – herpes simplex. Survivors can be left with minor or major deficits in function, either in localised or diffuse parts of the brain.

Tumours, cysts and abscesses

Tumours can develop in children and young people of any age. The second most common group of cancers in childhood are brain and spinal cord tumours, sometimes referred to as CNS or central nervous system tumours. They account for more than a quarter of all childhood cancers (Cancer Research UK, www.cancerresearchuk.org) – the most common childhood cancer is leukaemia, cancer of the blood-forming cells. Tumours are sometimes very small and slow growing, but sometimes develop into extremely large masses at an alarming rate. Regardless of whether these are malignant – cancerous – or benign growths, the fact that they grow within the skull or the brain itself, compressing and invading healthy tissue and taking up space and blood supply, can cause damage. Tumours in certain areas can also affect hormonal and chemical balances, further impairing brain function.

Cysts or **abscesses** are rare but can form in or next to the brain. An abscess is caused by an infection in a localised area which may result from bacteria, viruses or fungi, although bacterial infection is the most common. They can enter from the site of an infection – e.g. ear, sinus or tooth – and travel through the bloodstream or enter through an open head wound. Apart from the infection itself, these occupy space and can physically damage the brain as a result of their size. A cyst is a fluid-filled sac that can be present from birth and may never cause problems. However, these may cause difficulties and require treatment if, for instance, they increase in size, bleed or block the flow of CSF.

On occasions, vital surgery to remove such growths may, in itself, cause some unavoidable damage to the brain. Other treatments, such as radiotherapy, may also cause secondary damage, and it is for this reason that such treatments are rarely used on the brains of very young children.

Haemorrhage, thrombosis and hydrocephalus

These can all be caused by abnormalities or malformations within the structures of the brain and its blood supply.

The result of haemorrhage – bleeding from a ruptured blood vessel – and thrombosis – a clot in a blood vessel – can be a stroke, which is more commonly associated with the middle aged and elderly. However, this event, causing restriction of blood supply and therefore oxygen to a particular part of the brain, although rare, can occur in children and adolescents as well as in adults. A haemorrhage may result from a number of causes, but there are a small number of young people who have one or a number of malformations of small areas of artery walls within the brain – causing the wall to bulge like a balloon and, therefore, be weaker. These are called **aneurysms**. These may cause the artery to rupture suddenly and result in bleeding into or next to the brain. There are other vascular malformations that can damage the brain by causing bleeding, such as ones called **arteriovenous malformations (AVM)**.

Any obstruction to the flow of fluid that circulates around the brain and spinal cord – the **cerebrospinal fluid (CSF)** – can cause a build-up of this fluid within the ventricles of the brain, known as **hydrocephalus**. This can be a secondary result of illness or injury, but can also result from congenital malformation. This increased level of fluid, and therefore pressure, can cause damage to the delicate tissue of the brain. This may be treated by inserting a fine tube from a ventricle of the brain to the abdominal cavity to allow excess fluid to drain away. This is called a **ventriculoperitoneal** or **VP shunt**. Occasionally, the other end of the tube leads to the chest, rather than the abdominal cavity. Alternatively, this may be treated by the insertion of one or more drainage holes in strategic points at the base of a ventricle through which the excess fluid may drain. This is termed an **endoscopic third ventriculostomy (ETV)**. Hydrocephalus may be associated with injury to the brain, either because of the underlying cause of the hydrocephalus, or because of pressure of the excess fluid in the brain.

Other illnesses affecting brain function

A range of other illnesses may, on rare occasions, affect the supply of blood or oxygen to the brain or disrupt the delicate chemical balance of the body, thus causing damage. For instance, such injury is occasionally seen: after coma induced by illnesses such as diabetes, after continuous uncontrolled epileptic seizures **(status epilepticus)**, after a severe asthma attack or following illnesses causing heart failure.

Degenerative diseases

There is a range of degenerative neurological illnesses that, although rare in childhood, are characterised by the continuing progression of the symptoms. These illnesses include those provoking degeneration of the nerve cells and their fibres, e.g. genetic chemical disorders, Creutzfeldt-Jakob disease, and those provoked by an allergic reaction to vaccine. The effects of degenerative conditions are not addressed here as the purpose of this book is to consider the educational needs of children and young people who have recovered from the acute stage of illness or injury and are left with a non-progressive, acquired injury to the brain.

Effects

Clearly, there may be differences between injuries as a result of different causes and each individual case is unique and inherently different. However, these will be explained in general terms as this is not a medical textbook and is intended to provide background information on acquired brain injury for those involved with a young person's education.

Medical professionals often refer to primary and secondary injuries – often termed **insults** – to the brain after a trauma. This means injuries that are sustained at the moment when the accident or illness first occurs, i.e. primary injuries, and those that occur after this time, as a secondary result of the initial incident. Doctors are aware that by the time they see the patient, there is nothing that they can do to prevent the primary injuries that have already occurred. Their efforts, therefore, are focused on minimising the effects of these and, as far as possible, preventing the occurrence or severity of secondary insults.

The primary effects of brain injury

Primary insults to the brain include physical damage to or destruction of areas of the brain in penetrating injuries. Anything that prevents oxygen from reaching all or part of the brain, e.g. asphyxiation or haemorrhage, also results in the destruction of brain cells – **neurons**. Although this largely represents permanent loss, as mentioned in Chapter 1, recent research indicates that, contrary to previous understanding, there are some areas of the brain in which new cells may grow (Smith 2002).

Even without significant damage to the skull, an injury caused by external forces can produce a variety of immediate results.

Contusion

Contusion is the medical name for bruising and this will occur in brain tissue as in any other. The brain has room to move within the solid box of the skull that encases it and, particularly in the case of road traffic accidents, the brain may collide at speed with the front of the skull and then bounce off against the back. The inside of the skull is ridged and uneven in some places, particularly the frontal regions, and the brain tissue can be bruised or torn by this impact.

Haemorrhage

More significant bleeding, or haemorrhage, can also occur. Unlike bleeding on the outside of the body, blood inside the skull has nowhere to drain and can accumulate as an increasing-sized clot or **haematoma**. This will compress surrounding tissue and increase pressure within the skull unless it is removed. Bleeding like this also compromises flow of blood and, therefore, nutrients. Surgeons use different terminology to describe a haematoma depending on its location: intracranial – within the skull; extradural – on or over the outermost covering of the brain; subdural – between the outer coverings of the brain; or intracerebral – when bleeding extends into the brain.

Shearing

The brain is made up of many different structures and has a jelly-like consistency with fluid-filled spaces. These structures within the brain are of different sizes and densities. If the brain is shaken inside the skull during an accident, these structures will, therefore, move at slightly different speeds. The brain derives from a relatively small base – where the spinal cord enters the skull and joins the brainstem – and it may also rotate from this fixed point, as well as moving backwards and forwards inside the skull. As explained in Chapter 1, the brain operates as a result of the vast number of delicate connections within it, from cell to cell and from one area of the brain to another. As the brain is shaken or twisted in this fashion, these connections can break or **shear**.

The connections between brain cells involving axons, which enable communication via neural networks, can be severely disrupted. Severed axons, unlike most damaged neurons, can regrow and may effectively reinstate a damaged pathway. However, they do not always regrow correctly or as efficiently and also misconnections can be created. As described previously, when significant shearing has occurred throughout the brain, this is described as a **diffuse axonal injury**.

Coma

This is the term used to describe someone who is not responsive to external stimuli, i.e. not conscious or aware. Emergency medical services use a standardised measure called the **Glasgow Coma Scale (GCS)** to assess the extent of impairment of consciousness in adults and the **Paediatric Glasgow Coma Scale** in children. There are some limitations in the use of this for pre-verbal children.

Concussion

This is a term that describes a usually temporary condition after what may be a mild brain injury. Recent years have seen a great deal of research and interest in mild injuries (mTBI), and this has shown the potential long-term effects of this which were previously unrecognised (see Chapter 13 for detailed information).

The secondary effects of brain injury

Hypoxia

Recently damaged brain tissue is very sensitive to the effects of lack of oxygen – hypoxia. This may come about after the primary injury because the young person's airway becomes blocked or if he has very low blood pressure because of blood loss from other injuries – 'shock'.

Haemorrhage

It is possible that first or further haemorrhage can occur some time after the initial injury. This is a major reason why those attending hospital following an acquired brain injury, who seem well and are allowed home, are given advice to return immediately at the onset of specific symptoms. Untreated cerebral haemorrhage is very serious and possibly life threatening.

Oedema

Oedema is an excessive accumulation of fluid within tissue. We all know that if you injure another part of your body, such as your ankle, it will often begin to swell some time later. This causes no particular additional complications and it can be rested until the swelling subsides. However, swelling within the fixed space of the skull is a very different matter. If the whole brain swells, pressure builds up within the skull and the brain itself can suffer further damage, possibly to a fatal extent. If part of the brain swells, damage also occurs as it increasingly compresses the remainder, which can destroy cells or cause further shearing injuries. Such swelling can be provoked by both injuries and illnesses.

One of the main tasks for doctors immediately following a significant brain injury or the onset of a neurological illness is to monitor and attempt to control the pressure inside the skull. **Raised intracranial pressure** is a major cause of secondary brain damage and one reason why some patients die subsequent to the initial injury or onset of illness. The fact that doctors are more able to control this now has been a significant contributor towards the greater number of survivors of neurological illness and injury (Forsyth and Kirkham 2012).

Doctors may make a hole in the skull to insert a monitor in order to constantly check this pressure. Following serious brain injury, young people are often placed on a ventilator so that their oxygen intake can be carefully controlled. If the brain is not fully oxygenated, the automatic mechanism that reduces the build-up of fluid can fail very quickly and the brain can start to swell. As the intracranial pressure rises, the blood pressure is reduced, causing less cerebral circulation and, therefore, higher pressure, in a vicious circle of increasing symptoms.

Some acute centres also elect to sedate children and young people with severe brain injuries and to cool their core body temperature, for a number of clinical reasons (Flower and Hellings 2012).

Infection

Following a head injury, there is a risk of subsequent secondary infection after the event. This may be meningitis, spread via an open wound in the skull, or could be infection to other parts of the body secondary to intensive initial treatment. Chest infections are not uncommon in children and young people with traumatic brain injuries during the acute stage.

Post-traumatic epilepsy

It is sometimes the case that a person will suffer one or more seizures immediately after an injury to the brain or following the onset of a neurological infection. Seizures in the first few days after an injury may possibly cause further brain damage, but not necessarily. Seizures following traumatic brain injury are not uncommon and may be the only ones that a young person suffers. This does not mean that he has epilepsy or will go on to develop this. However, any person who has suffered a significant injury to the brain is initially under an increased risk of subsequently developing post-traumatic epilepsy. There is a further increased risk for those who have suffered a penetrating injury or a depressed skull fracture, where the outer coverings of the brain have been infiltrated. Epilepsy can develop weeks, months or even years after the original injury, although this risk gradually decreases over time. Eventually, if this has not happened, the young person's risk of developing epilepsy returns to that of the normal population.

Some people, for instance some of those who have a relatively early onset of post-traumatic epilepsy after the injury, will recover from this and stop experiencing seizures.

However, others will suffer from this permanently. Epilepsy, of course, can usually be controlled by appropriate medication.

Brain damage

Anything that causes an insult to the brain – be it a heavy blow or invasion of an infectious or other organism – can have a dramatic and significant effect on its ability to function normally. Other parts of our bodies, if damaged or infected, will bruise, swell, bleed or become inflamed, but the difference with damage to the brain is that, unlike the situation with bones, skin or muscles:

- Our ability to renew brain cells is limited.
- New and renewed connections between cells can be unpredictable.
- The brain has such a crucial role with regard to all other physical and cognitive functions still developing in a young person.
- It is hidden away inside the skull – you cannot see damage to a brain!

It is important to put the emotive term 'brain damage' into perspective: any bump on the head could damage or destroy some brain cells. Many of us may have suffered very minor cerebral contusions of which we are unaware. With a more significant injury or illness, as we are considering here, the child or young person will have suffered more damage to the brain. Unfortunately, the usual perception or understanding of this term has no foundation in these facts and it is often used as synonymous with very significant global intellectual, and possibly physical, impairment. The popular press and film-makers perpetuate this by emphasising the key question on everyone's lips after a significant accident to a loved one: 'Has he got brain damage?' by which they often mean, 'Will he be permanently unresponsive or severely mentally disabled?'

Unfortunately, therefore, people often see this issue as a clear case of two options. The person will either 'recover', i.e. revert completely back to how they were before, or be 'brain damaged', i.e. completely incapacitated. This is very far from the truth and anyone who has a child with an acquired brain injury will assure you that, far from being clearly black and white, the grey area is extensive.

Stages of recovery

In terms of the results of trauma to the brain, there are many medical and rehabilitation models by which severity of injury and recovery are considered and assessed. From the point of view of families and those working with the young person in education, we can consider this in three stages. The first is the acute stage, just after the accident or onset of the illness; the second is the initial period of recovery; and the third is from that time onwards.

It is useful to have an awareness of the earlier stages even if you do not encounter the young person and his family until later in this process. Understanding of what will have gone before can raise awareness of the issues and help us to understand the young person and family in the longer term. It is also important to recognise the third, ongoing, phase of continued recovery in terms of manifestation of deficit and capacity for rehabilitation; the effects of acquired brain injury for the child or adolescent and his family do not end when he has 'recovered' in medical terms. This is a different beginning.

Acute stage

When a child or young person first suffers an insult to the brain, it is an extremely traumatic time for him and his family. In more minor cases, he may have a concussion or be confused and disorientated. If he has been involved in an accident, he may have other injuries as well, such as cuts or broken bones. With more significant brain injuries, the young person may be unconscious. He may well be sedated and ventilated, and it can be difficult to understand the nature of his conscious state when he is being kept under sedation. Parents may have been told that the prognosis for their child is unclear or even bleak.

Once the young person has stabilised, if he has been sedated, doctors will allow him to wake up and to breathe for himself, but the priority is to minimise existing damage and to attempt to prevent further damage occurring. If he is suffering from an illness or infection, treatment for this will start as soon as possible.

This is a very confusing and bewildering time for other members of the family. If the young person has been involved in an accident, they or other family members may also have been injured. Parents may be overwhelmed by a variety of emotions, for instance fear or guilt. They will feel frustration if the doctors and nurses cannot accurately predict the outcome at this early stage.

Early recovery

Once the young person is out of danger and his condition has been stabilised, the often lengthy process of recovery or rehabilitation can begin.

Young people, particularly those who have been in coma for some time, may return to consciousness gradually. They may begin to respond, for instance to voices and to obey commands, e.g. to move a hand, intermittently. They are not considered to be out of coma until they are responding consistently.

Any inflammation and bruising will take some time to subside. This certainly often does not happen before the young person is seen to 'wake up', which is another myth perpetuated by the media. In films, we so often see anxious relatives surrounding the person in coma, who may be swathed in bandages and linked to a bank of machinery.

Regardless of the length of time that this is supposed to have continued, we witness the moment when they open their eyes, recognise and speak to their loved ones, and drop gently off to sleep before waking to resume their normal lives. You will not be surprised to hear that this does not happen in real life!

After a severe injury, the reality is that, at this stage, children – or adults – may not recognise anyone around them, may not be continent, may be unable to speak and may have no control over their movements. Bruising, inflammation and severed connections are preventing the brain from functioning normally. It may be apparent that the young person has either very tight or very floppy muscles – referred to as alteration of **muscle tone** – all over or on one side of the body, preventing movement on that side.

As the child or young person seems gradually to become more awake or more aware, he may seem distressingly agitated or anxious. He may struggle and toss about as if upset or in pain. When he begins to make sounds, it may be to cry out or to moan. This is very disconcerting for the family, although the young person will not remember this later.

It can be even more worrying for the family when their child begins to speak, as he may appear to have lost his inhibitions and shout out in an embarrassing way. This can include swearing and cursing, with the young person having lost all awareness of social rules. He may be disinhibited and throw off his clothing or masturbate publicly.

This can be likened to a major regression, when an older child or young adult behaves like a baby or toddler. It is as if some basic processes and needs continue to function, but without the benefit of refinement and maturation that have previously occurred as the child grew up.

Not only can this be very upsetting for the family, but it can also be very difficult for the young person's friends to cope with if they see him in hospital. Teachers frequently visit with groups of peers, and it is important to find out what state the injured or ill person is in beforehand to fully inform the other students about what to expect. They may feel embarrassed about talking to their classmate if he does not seem aware, or unsure how to respond if he is shouting. It is also important to allow these other students time to talk through their feelings afterwards.

It is sometimes suggested that classmates make an audio or video recording to send to their injured friend to assist with his recovery. This can be done from an early stage and may help, even if the injured youngster does not seem to be aware enough to be able to see or hear this.

Not all brain-injured young people go through this stage. Some may seem to recover to their previous state much more quickly, while others gradually regain awareness in a much quieter fashion, although they may have initial physical difficulties or problems with speech, eating or drinking.

There is frequently a variable length of time, after consciousness is regained, when the young person appears to be aware, but it becomes apparent that he has no continuous memory for events. This is referred to as a period of **post-traumatic amnesia (PTA)**. This period of amnesia is 'lost' forever, and in older children and young adults it can be used at any time in the future as a guide to the severity of the initial injury and to the likelihood of future neuropsychological problems.

For those whose early symptoms are severe or seem to indicate hopelessness to family and friends, the future can look very bleak. Often doctors will be reluctant to give a specific prognosis in the early stages because it can be impossible to predict the extent to which a young person will recover. However, when he then does show signs of recovery and of regaining previous functions, initial progress can be quite rapid.

It is very common to see parents' hopes change rapidly and they continually alter their aspirations. When their child initially appears so badly injured, often their only hope is that he will live, regardless of any disability. The often dramatic recovery process injects a gradually increasing level of hope into their minds. 'If only he can live' can quickly change to 'If only he can speak' and, just as rapidly, to 'If only he can walk', as the previous goals are often quite rapidly achieved. Naturally, family and friends then begin to assume that this rate of recovery will continue until the young person is totally back to normal. The press, again, fuels this belief as we see dramatic headlines, proclaiming 'Miracle recovery!' Certainly, it is miraculous to see the ways in which the brain recovers from a major assault on its function, but this type of rapid early recovery is to be expected and is not unique.

After this very rapid stage of change, progress does slow down and further recovery takes place at a slower rate. Happily, some young people do recover completely and can be said to be 'back to normal'. Unfortunately, though, the majority of those who have sustained significant brain injuries, and some of those with mild ones, will continue to experience a level of acquired difficulties which, for many, will be present for the rest of their lives.

Many parents are understandably very anxious to leave hospital with their child and to return to their normal lives. Most are so grateful that their child has survived and is recovering that they do not contemplate significant future problems. A few of these young people will transfer to specialist rehabilitation facilities, but most will be discharged home and return to education relatively quickly. The third stage of recovery then begins.

Further recovery and rehabilitation

Many parents say that it is not until they have returned home and are attempting to get back to normal that they begin to realise that the effects of their child's injury are still significant. Unfortunately, as time passes, many realise that the child they now have is very different from the one they knew before. This can be a strange and unnerving situation, as so many of these young people make good physical recoveries and look just as they did previously. Despite possible early difficulties with speech, this frequently recovers to an adequate conversational level. It is often the case, therefore, that other people do not recognise the differences and presume that the young person has recovered, expecting the same behaviour and abilities as before. Relatives, friends, teachers and others make these assumptions and parents can feel very isolated and unsupported when attempting to face a confusing situation. They may be the only ones who realise that they have brought home a changed or different person from the hospital. Young people with acquired brain injury often carry no 'badge of disability'.

The reality is that these young people have sustained brain damage, however difficult or emotive that term may be. It does not mean that they will necessarily have any physical impairment and it does not mean that, with appropriate support, they will not be able to achieve academically or experience a good quality of life. It does mean that for years after the injury, they will still be going through a process of change and development, which may include some recovery of skills affected by the injury. A serious injury to any part of the body will usually require some form of rehabilitation. This also applies to the brain, but this is a much longer process for a child or adolescent. It is also the case that, unlike a damaged limb that may require physical rehabilitation, damage to the brain causes cognitive difficulties for which the most appropriate rehabilitation is largely within educational settings.

References

Flower, O. and Hellings, S. (2012) 'Sedation in traumatic brain injury'. *Emergency Medicine International* 2012 Article ID 637171, p. 11.

Forsyth, R. and Kirkham, F. (2012) 'Predicting outcome after childhood brain injury'. *CMAJ: Canadian Medical Association Journal* 184 (11), pp. 1257–1264.

Reed, J., Byard, K. and Fine, H. (2015) 'Introduction', in Reed, J., Byard, K. and Fine, H. (eds) *Neuropsychological Rehabilitation of Childhood Brain Injury*. Basingstoke: Palgrave Macmillan, pp. 1–5.

Semrud-Clikeman, M. (2007) *Social Competence in Children*. New York: Springer Science & Business Media.

Smith, A. (2002) *The Brain's Behind It*. Stafford: Network Educational Press.

Why does ABI provoke different special educational needs?

A wide range of acquired deficits might impact on ability to access learning. The presence of subtle but highly significant deficits in executive functioning, working memory, attention or learning might be more difficult for educators to identify or understand.

(Gracey et al. 2015)

ABI presents a challenge for schools and colleges because the resultant difficulties are not well recognised.

> Everyone thinks that Mark is fine because he looks so good; he is walking and talking, and that is all they have the time to see. We seem to be the only ones who understand that he is not the same as he was before his accident. He may look the same on the outside but he is a different person inside. Everything about him – the things he says and does – are nothing like how they were before. That's the hardest thing, knowing that you've got a different child and not being able to talk about it because no one understands. They don't want to know. Your child looks healthy so what are you complaining about? Sometimes I think it's me that is going mad.
> (Parent of a 12-year-old boy)

Research indicates that children and young people with ABI often require some educational approaches that are different from those commonly or traditionally used (e.g. Ylvisaker et al. 2005; Hawley 2005).

Acquired brain injuries commonly involve diffuse damage, and it is often the combination and complexity of this which results in unusual profiles of learning and behaving.

The crucial issue is that the **processes for learning** may be impaired. Regrettably, too many educators focus on what is visible or obvious, and too few make the connection between an ABI and the disruption to the underlying brain functions that affect learning potential and abilities. If they do see sudden changes as a result of a known injury, they may not know why they have occurred, and even if they are aware of an earlier injury they may fail to associate current difficulties with a neurological event that happened months or years ago.

Young people with ABI may share a number of similar characteristics with other students who have learning difficulties, but there are differences that are important to acknowledge because different and/or additional strategies or supports are often required for helping students with ABI to learn and behave appropriately in the classroom. Failure to recognise and accommodate the differences can seriously compromise a student's progress, exacerbate existing difficulties, and increase the likelihood of secondary learning and/or behavioural problems. Important basic information for education staff to know is how the needs of a student who has suffered an ABI may differ from those of others.

Students with ABI have different special needs because:

- **They have had a period of 'normal' growth and development**. Injury and subsequent disability occurs suddenly after a period of normal development. They have often had previous successful experiences academically and socially and may remember these very well. Their perceptions of the differences between present and previous abilities and coping with their sudden loss – of anticipated levels of achievement, of activities, of friends, of skill level, of methods of working – can lead to psychosocial problems such as frustration, anger, depression, withdrawal and/or denial.

- **They often maintain a pre-injury self-concept**. Not surprisingly, many people with injured brains cannot easily analyse their own dysfunction. They have great difficulties in understanding their brain injury and the changes to their abilities. They see themselves as they were before; they expect to be able to carry out the same social and academic activities as the peers they identified with prior to their injury. Gradual rejection by that peer group and subsequent isolation and loneliness are commonly reported. They may be resistant to different strategies for learning because they are familiar with and wish to use strategies which have been successful for them pre-injury.

- **There are often significant discrepancies in ability levels**. They may retain or recover some skills achieved prior to injury but not regain others, so resulting in very unusual profiles of learning skills. They may retain good abilities related to areas unaffected by the injury but have lost skills normally required to demonstrate these – e.g. a student may have excellent vocabulary knowledge but lack organisational skills to formulate expressive language to an age-appropriate level.

- **There are marked contrasts between pre-and post-injury capabilities**. Acquisition of new learning is most problematic following an ABI. This is a very important feature that creates an unusual profile, which is very different from other young people. They may have learnt and retained skills and information acquired prior to injury, which may seem to be inconsistent with their present slow speed of processing information and significant memory difficulties. Children and young people may score at misleadingly high levels on conventional tests of intelligence or knowledge because of the information and skills learnt prior to injury, so creating an impression of ongoing competence to achieve academically. They may achieve to age-equivalent levels initially, but as new learning is impaired, they gradually fall behind their peers.

- **They have an academic and behavioural profile that changes frequently**. The rate at which change can occur and the pattern of academic and behavioural functioning over time can be very different from most students with learning disabilities. This is associated, in part, with neurological recovery. There can be unpredictable and uneven recovery or progress both on a day-to-day basis as well as over a longer term. They can seem to be learning rather rapidly at times and yet there are other times when there appears to be a plateau effect. They can 'grow out' of problems as they recover skills or compensate for impaired ones.

- **There may be delayed deficits**. A young person's brain is still developing and the impact of damage may become apparent even years after the injury occurred. There may be injury to a part of the brain that is responsible for skills that do not mature until later within the developmental process and therefore future age-appropriate skills then fail to emerge. Even if an injury has occurred in early childhood, it is sometimes not until adolescence that certain difficulties manifest themselves when expected abilities to cope with increasing or different academic and social demands do not develop. Due to the time that has elapsed between the occurrence of the injury and the emerging learning or behavioural difficulties, there is commonly no association made between the current concerns and the ABI.

- **Family members experience an ongoing grieving process**. 'This mourning is complicated by the reality that, in one important sense, there was no loss – the child has lived' (Ylvisaker 1998). Parents may mourn the loss of the child they knew. Plans for the future and educational goals that their child's development prior to injury had led them to anticipate may have to be re-evaluated. It can be difficult for others who did not know the young person or family prior to injury to appreciate the enormity of the effects; a brain injury to a child is an injury that reverberates throughout the whole family. Making plans and decisions about any special educational arrangements can be confusing and a considerable source of distress and anxiety for parents at a time when they may already be emotionally overloaded.

References

Gracey, F., Olsen, G., Austin, L., Watson, S. and Malley, D. (2015) 'Integrating psychological therapy into interdisciplinary child neuropsychological rehabilitation', in Reed, J., Byard, K. and Fine, H. (eds) *Neuropsychological Rehabilitation of Childhood Brain Injury*. Basingstoke: Palgrave Macmillan, pp. 191–214.

Hawley, C. A. (2005) 'Saint or sinner? Teacher perceptions of a child with brain injury'. *Pediatric Rehabilitation* 8 (2), pp. 117–129.

Ylvisaker, M. (ed) (1998) *Traumatic Brain Injury Rehabilitation: Children and Adolescents*, 2nd edn. Boston, MA: Butterworth-Heinemann.

Ylvisaker, M., Turkstra, L. and Coelho, C. (2005) 'Behavioral and social interventions for individuals with traumatic brain injury: A summary of the research with clinical implications'. *Seminars in Speech & Language* 26 (4), pp. 256–267.

Most common areas of difficulty provoked by ABI

We can think of our cognitive system as working in much the same way as a very advanced hi-fi system, which comes as a total package but is made up of a variety of individual parts. . . . A head injury is the equivalent of shaking up this very complex delicate hi-fi system; some parts will be damaged, other parts may work perfectly well. It is important to understand which parts are working and which parts are faulty.

(Powell 1994)

Subtle or significant damage can be caused unpredictably to specific or diverse areas of the brain as a result of accident or injury. Small or large groups of neurons may be destroyed, or it may be those all-important connections between them that are damaged. New connections can be created, but these may not be as efficient or may be created at the expense of others. Damage to neurons whose connections were not mature and developed may affect future maturation and skill development. In contrast, some areas of the brain may be unaffected or new connections may be efficiently formed to restore or to provoke efficient development of specific skills.

This means that every acquired brain injury results in a unique pattern of strengths and weaknesses, which is frequently complex and unusual and which evolves as a young person matures. However, there are some skills that are most commonly affected by an acquired brain injury. It is important to have an understanding of these and the ways in which they may be affected in order to identify or to address them in educational settings. Difficulties in these areas may be present in any combination – it is unlikely that all will be affected – and within a limitless range of severity.

The following descriptions mainly refer to difficulties that can be provoked by the organic injury, i.e. damage to the brain. The young person's reactions to these acquired difficulties can cause additional difficulties that will be discussed separately.

It will be primarily the cognitive impairments that affect a student's learning ability, but physical, sensory, behavioural, social and emotional problems will also impact on curricular access and academic progress. These are, therefore, also addressed here and in Chapters 7 and 8.

Physical and sensory effects

Many young people who have an acquired brain injury may appear to make a relatively good physical recovery. A smaller percentage are left with obvious motor – physical – impairments. Young people typically demonstrate a faster and greater recovery of physical skills than of other areas of functioning. This can often lead to false assumptions being made; a relatively speedy recovery of obvious gross motor impairment can encourage a belief that recovery of all other functions will be commensurate with the physical gains. However, this is frequently not the case.

However, there may also be less easily observable but ongoing physical deficits, which are by no means inconsequential – such as those relating to balance and co-ordination or those relating to bladder control. Some subtle impairments can have considerable impact on a student's ability to learn and to feel fully accepted by and integrated with his peers. There is also no predictable or reliable pattern of recovery. Some functions may return quickly and completely, others may partially recover slowly, while some physical deficits may be permanent.

Essential to addressing motor skill deficits are the assessments and any subsequent intervention and advice from physiotherapists and occupational therapists.

Motor skills

Injury to the parts of the brain that regulate movement, posture and co-ordination result in gross and/or fine motor difficulties. **Gross motor skills** are the large movements which commonly involve the whole body, e.g. running, walking, jumping, throwing, catching, etc. **Fine motor skills** are the smaller movements, mainly of the hands, for activities involving manipulating, pointing or holding objects, e.g. when using a knife and fork, pencil, scissors, etc.

Motor deficits can range in severity. Total paralysis of large muscle groups, such as **quadriplegia** – paralysis in all four limbs – and **hemiplegia** or **hemiparesis** – motor weakness or paralysis on one side of the body – can severely restrict movement and necessitate the use of a wheelchair or other physical aid. Total paralysis affects only very few young people after an ABI; the majority recover motor skills to a point where independent functioning can occur.

More subtle difficulties can result in tremors and poor balance, or problems with motor planning, i.e. the ability to select the required movements in a particular sequence, and motor co-ordination. **Ataxia** involves the loss of ability to efficiently co-ordinate movements, which can also result in problems with balance and unsteadiness, i.e. shakiness.

Speed of movement and reaction times may be reduced after an ABI, affecting swiftness and co-ordination which may previously have been apparent, for example in sporting activities or playing musical instruments.

Loss of full hand function can sometimes result, making it necessary to learn to carry out daily tasks mainly using only one hand or with reduced function in a previously dominant one. Handwriting with the non-dominant hand can be difficult, frustrating and time consuming, particularly for older children. Young people who continue to have movement in their affected arm and/or hand but find this effortful may need frequent encouragement to use it in order not to allow further deterioration of function. They may also ignore affected limbs and be very reluctant to use them because of deficits in sensory feedback.

Abnormalities of muscle tone may occur after ABI. Muscle tone refers to the amount of tension or resistance to movement in a muscle. This enables us to keep our bodies in certain positions and to make smooth, co-ordinated movements. The tone changes when movement occurs. For example, to lift a hand, the biceps muscles on the front of the arm need to shorten – so increasing the tone – at the same time as the triceps muscles on the back of the arm are lengthened – so reducing the tone. To be able to carry out a movement smoothly, the tone in the muscle groups must be co-ordinated. An injured brain may no longer be able to send appropriate messages to each muscle group, so restricting the range and type of movement of body parts and joints.

Sensory impairments

A brain injury can disrupt any part of the sensory system that transmits or processes sensory information – sight, hearing, smell, taste or touch. **Sensory integration** is the combination and interpretation by the brain of information from different senses relating to one's own body and the environment around it.

Problems with **proprioception** are difficulties understanding where limbs are in relation to the rest of the body and to the space around.

Sensory systems are subsumed within many parts of the brain, which is why complete loss of function relating to any one sense occurs infrequently following ABI, but also why some disturbance is not uncommon. Some sensory problems resolve gradually, whereas others may be permanent. Visual and hearing impairments have obvious and profound implications for learning and socialising.

Visual difficulties

Following ABI, there can be problems with vision – i.e. the ability to see – or visual perception – i.e. the ability to understand what is seen – or both. Problems are not usually the result of damage to the eyes themselves – although, of course, this can occur – but to the extensive visual system, which is widely spread across the brain, from the eyes themselves along visual pathways to the occipital lobes, which are at the back of the brain. Consequently, ABI can cause problems associated with the following:

- **Tracking** – the ability of the eye to track smoothly across a page of print, or to follow a moving object
- **Focus change** – looking quickly from near to distance without any blurring
- **Binocularity** – using information from both eyes in a co-ordinated way to enable depth and accurate movement perception
- **Fixation** – locating and focusing on a series of stationary objects quickly and accurately – (e.g. words when reading)
- **Visual fields** – the total area that can be seen without moving the eyes or head
- **Visual acuity** – ability to see at varying distances
- **Visual perception** – how visual information is interpreted in the brain (discussed in more detail in a separate section)

Or, it can provoke the following:

- **Visual neglect** – neglect or inattention to visual information located on one side of the body; this can occur despite intact vision and is considered an attentional deficit
- **Diplopia** – double vision

It is very easy for visual disturbances to go undetected, and common for young people who experience them to be either unaware of the extent of their visual limitations through adaptation to them, or to try and ignore them. Spectacles may help rectify or ameliorate some but not all visual problems resulting from ABI.

Hearing impairments

These can create a feeling of isolation for a student and may be very difficult to adjust to if he has no previous history of these. The ability to speak clearly is often retained, especially if expressive language was already well developed prior to injury. However, a student may no longer have the capacity for checking the accuracy of his own speech, and therapy may be required. Students who can speak clearly and who may have some lip-reading skills may be easily overlooked in the classroom. Assistive technological devices such as hearing aids can help a young person to locate sound, understand the spoken word and undertake many daily and leisure activities.

Fatigue and loss of stamina

Problems with fatigue and sleep are a common part of the recovery process immediately following ABI. However, although they often improve over time after the injury, they can continue to be of long-term concern as they interfere with a young person's general level of activity and functioning in the educational setting. They have a significant impact on learning because they may affect everything a student does and can be a contributory factor in cognitive dysfunction, irritability, depression and anxiety.

Fatigue

This affects all aspects of a young person's functioning at school or college. Energy levels for both mental and physical activity can rapidly decrease, and tiredness can overpower much more quickly and extremely than most people experience. This can in turn affect frustration tolerance and behaviour. Even if there are no obvious physical changes following an ABI, children and adolescents can become easily tired due to the huge effort necessary to carry out tasks that may well have been completed with little or no difficulty prior to injury. Fatigue and sleep disorders are often not well understood and a recommendation for the young person to go to bed earlier is not necessarily the answer – if only it could be that simple! Powell (1994) reports individuals with ABI who have used the analogy of a car running out of petrol: 'very suddenly there is no energy in the tank and you have to stop'.

Many family members report fatigue to be one of the most common and longer-term problems after ABI. Fatigue can be either physical or mental but they are closely related, and people with ABI frequently experience a combination of both, but not necessarily at the same time. Mental fatigue may result in a student having limited capacity to stay on task in the classroom, without any evidence of physical fatigue. Although a young person may be deemed ready to return to education after injury, fatigue often continues to be a limiting factor for the extent to which he is able to actively participate. A huge amount of effort may be necessary to complete the simplest of tasks. He may have to work much harder to get a fraction of the work done that he achieved prior to his injury. This greater expending of energy then compounds the student's existing difficulties, making everything else so much more effortful.

Indications of fatigue can be manifested in a range of functions, such as:

- deterioration in balance or co-ordination of movements – e.g. walking in a floppy or haphazard way, or dragging a foot
- deterioration in posture – e.g. may slump across the desk or table
- excessive yawning
- complaints of headaches
- inability to attend and concentrate
- difficulty sustaining a level of performance
- reduced output of work and decreased accuracy
- deterioration in behaviour or compliance

Medication for seizures, pain or other conditions may also have an effect on fatigue and energy levels.

Making allowances for fatigue can be considered disruptive to class activities, and some members of teaching staff may believe that the behaviour is just laziness. Flexibility and patience are needed! Without understanding of the cause of this, an approach to managing the flagging competence of a tired student may be with encouragement to 'just do a little bit more'. However, many students with ABI are frequently not able to summon up additional resources of energy to make this happen, and any pressure for continued effort which they are unable to generate can have a negative effect on their behaviour and motivation.

Sleep disturbance

This also provokes fatigue. Most of us need a good night's sleep in order to function adequately, physically, cognitively and psychologically. However, this is often something that is difficult to achieve following an ABI, either as a direct result of the injury to parts of the brain that help to control or regulate sleep, or as an indirect result of the subsequent routine changes, or other injury-related symptoms (Ouellet et al. 2004). Sleep is a process that involves multiple parts of the brain. The states of sleep and wakefulness are the products of very finely tuned, interconnected and interdependent systems. Any disruption to these complex anatomical and biochemical systems, which are spread over wide areas of the brain, adversely affects the timing of sleep and the ability to stay awake, to fall asleep or to stay asleep.

Headaches

Headaches are a frequently reported symptom after an ABI (Sharp et al. 2006). They generally resolve with time, but it is important to monitor any changes in their severity or frequency and report them to the parents and doctor. Either continuous or intermittent headaches can dramatically affect a student's performance in tasks and increase irritability. The severity of headaches can be difficult to define, and may be related to one of a number of causes, e.g. fatigue, migraine or tension.

Post-traumatic epilepsy

Seizures occur when the normal functioning of the brain is disrupted by neurons firing electrical impulses in an excessive or disorderly way. Epilepsy refers to a condition marked by recurrent unprovoked seizures. It is not uncommon for people to suffer seizures immediately following a trauma to the brain, but when these occur within the first week, this is not classed as post-traumatic epilepsy and does not necessarily mean that the person will continue to experience seizures as a chronic condition (Gupta and Gupta 2006). When a person suffers one or more seizures after the first week post-trauma, this may be diagnosed as epilepsy. Seizures may occur as complications of any brain injury or be a symptom of many kinds of disorders or illnesses that can affect the brain, e.g. encephalitis or meningitis (Anderson et al. 2001).

There are many different types of epileptic seizure which may be focal – partial – or generalised, i.e. affecting part or all of the brain and involving loss of consciousness or not. Some seizures may involve jerking of the arms and legs and a loss of consciousness; others may cause involuntary movement of just one or two limbs with no loss of consciousness. Other forms of epilepsy may involve only momentary loss of consciousness, in which there may be no movement, or slight facial twitching or diminished consciousness with unusual or bizarre behaviour. Diagnosis of epilepsy is clinical and it needs to be based on detailed descriptions of events witnessed by others and experienced by the young person before, during and after what may be considered to be a seizure. Detailed information on types and management of epilepsy are available from organisations referred to in the resources section at the back of this book.

Bowel and bladder functions

Bowel and bladder control involves both physical and cognitive skills; it requires an awareness of the subtle physical signs of needing to go to the toilet and the ability to act on the signs. Acquired brain injury can affect continence in a number of ways, such as in terms of the urgency and frequency with which the person needs to pass a bowel or bladder movement. A medical and behavioural assessment may be required to ascertain the nature of the problem.

Hormonal changes

Although rare, these can occur following an ABI and can result in precocious or delayed puberty, or changes in growth rate. Secondary sexual characteristics may emerge before the normal time and there may be early onset of menstruation or voice change. This can be difficult for children to manage because the physical and emotional changes, and sexual interests and behaviour normally associated with puberty, are not only outside the range of experiences of the child's peer group, but considered inappropriate too.

Appetite and weight change

Weight gain or loss may follow acquired brain injury, for one or more of a number of reasons. Dietary intake during the acute stage of any illness is commonly disrupted and swallowing difficulties can also occur. Rapid increase in weight may result from damage to the part of the brain that controls appetite, so reducing the sense of satiation, although this problem is rare. Problems with weight gain are more often associated with motor impairments which restrict movements, resulting in fewer calories being required. Appetite and weight change can also be related to behavioural or cognitive changes and need to be clinically addressed.

Language and communication

There are many areas of our brains that have developed in order to enable us to process, to formulate and to functionally use language as communication in speech and writing. Although there are well-known, so-called language centres in the brain, quite different areas are involved when we hear, see, think, speak or write words. Foreign languages are processed in a slightly different area of the brain to that which processes a person's mother tongue (Dick et al. 2008).

The range of a child's developing vocabulary and his use of language are affected by his environment, but speech itself is part of normal development. The area of the brain primarily responsible for speech is, for most of us, on the left side. Following ABI, it is most usually the case that young people will retain or regain the ability to formulate basic speech. Superficially their language skills may, therefore, appear to be intact, but this does not mean that all of the more complex language processes are functioning, or will subsequently develop, normally.

The other language skills that most of us use for communication – reading and writing – do not develop naturally like speech, but have to be taught. Like speech, they are crucial to academic progress and achievement and the progress that a student has made in the development of these skills prior to an ABI is important. The ability to acquire new learning subsequent to an injury is more likely to be impaired.

Language skills are also closely linked with and reliant upon other skills, such as attention and memory. Many communication and language difficulties following acquired brain injury have their basis in specific cognitive impairment. The ability to speak and to 'hold his own' in normal conversation does not preclude underlying problems relating to communication and language ability.

Speech

Following an acquired brain injury, a young person may experience any of the following difficulties:

- **Dysphasia** – an impairment of the ability either to produce (expressive dysphasia) or to understand (receptive dysphasia) speech and language.
- **Dysarthria** – a condition affecting the muscles necessary to produce speech (Duffy 2012). This can vary considerably in severity from a mild degree of

slurring (sometimes only apparent when the person becomes tired) to virtual unintelligibility. Dysarthria does not impact on the understanding of language.

- **Verbal dyspraxia** – a condition affecting the use of muscles in a co-ordinated, sequential way in order to produce spoken language. This may appear to provoke similar problems to dysarthria. A person with verbal dyspraxia may also encounter difficulties controlling the rate and volume of their speech. This does not affect language comprehension.

- **Low volume** – Some of these young people have a 'weak' voice, only being able to speak relatively quietly, which may be linked to a lengthy period of assisted ventilation – breathing – in hospital.

- **Mild difficulties** – Young people whose speech shows improvement over time may be left with some mild difficulties, such as imprecise articulation, phonatory weakness, hypernasality, impaired prosody (and pitch variation) or difficulties with rate of speech (slow or rapid) (Ylvisaker et al. 1994).

Oral language

As previously mentioned, superficially the young person's use of expressive language may seem unimpaired. Many young people who had normal language development prior to their illness or injury recover the ability to form grammatically acceptable sentences and to use everyday language. They may also perform within normal limits in assessments that are formulated for those with developmental language problems. However, they may have difficulties in the areas listed below.

Word finding

This difficulty relates to the ability to recall specific words from memory, despite knowledge of the words they are unable to find. They will know the name for a person or object and be able to describe it, but sometimes will be unable to recall the correct name for it. This can be understandably frustrating. However, many people learn to mask this in normal speech and become very adept at talking around a subject or contriving to prompt their listener to provide the missing word for them. This also affects written language, but a young person can sometimes avoid specific vocabulary usage in context. However, when time is limited or specific vocabulary is required – for instance, during examinations – then their difficulty is all too apparent. Problems with word finding are also most pronounced when stressed, anxious or fatigued, and so the person will be further disadvantaged in, for instance, assessment, interviews, when feeling anxious or in unfamiliar situations. Individuals experience variations in the level of severity of their word-finding difficulties: for some, this represents an occasional problem, whereas for others it is very frequent.

Organisation

All aspects of organisational ability can be affected by ABI. This can specifically affect expressive language, resulting in rambling, tangential speech and an inability to formulate an argument or to stick to the point.

Information processing

Slowed speeds of information processing are relatively common following ABI and can affect expressive language. Some students need more time to think through what they wish to say, but unfortunately, this is not always possible. If a teacher asks a question of the whole class or group, the student with ABI may not be able to respond promptly. An answer may be blurted out minutes later, to the bemusement of peers and staff who have moved on from the previous topic. The student may also have missed much of what has been said in the intervening period while he was still processing the original question and formulating a response.

> Ann was always very slow to respond verbally when she returned to her primary school following a road traffic accident in which she suffered a significant brain injury. There was concern that she was becoming isolated and her peers and all adults in the school were encouraged to speak to her, even just to say hello, when they passed her in school. You could often hear people call out greetings as they rushed past. Unfortunately, by the time Ann managed to respond to these friendly comments, the people who initiated them had long gone and forgotten that they had never received a reply.

Perseveration

This means repetition of the same word, phrase or topic repeatedly and in an inappropriate way, as if they are 'stuck' within a particular thought and unable to move on. The person is often unaware that they are doing this.

Abstract thought

If a young person's ability to think imaginatively or to consider abstract ideas is impaired, his expressive language may be confined purely to factual information. Young people with acquired brain injuries – particularly with frontal lobe damage – may be very concrete thinkers.

Auditory receptive language

There may be difficulties understanding spoken language. If a person's speed of processing language is slow, much of what is said by others may be missed. This can be particularly apparent during conversations of children and adolescents, who often chat very rapidly. Other factors affecting understanding of language may relate to the following areas:

Vocabulary knowledge

A child's understanding and knowledge of vocabulary normally increases with maturity. As pre-existing knowledge is frequently preserved after an acquired brain injury, tests of receptive vocabulary knowledge relatively soon after such an injury may well show an age-appropriate level. However, as in other areas, failure to acquire new knowledge at an expected rate often provokes a subsequent widening gap between the vocabulary knowledge of the student with ABI and his peers. It is important to differentiate between vocabulary knowledge and access to this, i.e. word finding.

Quantity and complexity

Simple verbal information, or that presented in small amounts, may be understood, but lengthy or more complex communication can present significant difficulty. This also may be affected by the time available to process this and the rate at which it is delivered. A student may be able to understand information presented slowly and clearly, but not when the rate increases.

Higher-level language

Children's understanding of language may be unimpaired at a young age, but they may fail to develop the skills necessary to interpret or to understand more complex language forms as they mature. This is frequently related to lack of appropriate executive skill development and retention of a more immature form of concrete thinking. Young people with acquired brain injuries may be unable to understand subtle humour and sarcasm or abstract and indirect meaning. They may fail to understand figures of speech or metaphors. This only becomes significant when their peers develop such skills and when academic work becomes more abstract. When required to respond to questions, they may be able to answer factual ones but not those requiring deductive reasoning. Inability to 'read between the lines' or to understand nuances in conversation can present a significant impediment in social situations. Such difficulties are frequently referred to as **pragmatic language difficulties**. Pragmatics means the use of language in social and interactional contexts and an understanding of non-literal meanings.

Written language

It is important to consider the age and ability of the young person when he is injured and to take into account his level of literacy ability at that time. A child injured prior to the acquisition of basic literacy skills is likely to have more difficulty acquiring these than an older child who needs to regain them. However, there may well be difficulties extending skills learnt prior to injury. Some children and young people with ABI have very significant acquired difficulties relating to written language in contrast to their more efficient spoken language ability. Any one or a combination of motor, cognitive or sensory deficits can impact on this. Some common ones include:

- **Fine motor skills**. Impairment of these and visuo-spatial skills will obviously significantly affect the student's ability to make the co-ordinated movements necessary for writing.

- **Organisation**. Impairment of this skill will also impact on written work. The student whose spoken language is disorganised, rambling or verbose will produce similar written work. He may do well when required to write brief phrases or sentences, but be completely unable to plan or to organise longer or more complex pieces of written work.

- **Spelling**. Spelling problems are not uncommon in children and young people with acquired brain injuries, particularly for those who were injured at a relatively young age, before a sound knowledge base was established. This can relate to problems with auditory discrimination, but also to memory or sequencing skills or to phonological-processing ability.

- **Reading**. Students with ABI commonly experience much greater difficulty understanding that which they read than with actually reading the words. Reading tests that only assess word recognition may therefore indicate scores within average ranges, but this will not reflect an ability to read for meaning. They also sometimes have more difficulty than would be expected locating information when revisiting text. Their approach to this may be disorganised and inefficient.

Social communication

This is highlighted with reference to language because of its significance, but is addressed in more detail in Chapter 8. Difficulties can relate to:

- **Peer expectations**. Being party to the fast-moving jargon and abbreviations of teenage interactions is crucial to social acceptability at that age. Young people with ABI may not understand the humour used by their peers – or may misinterpret it and become the butt of jokes themselves – and may take comments very literally, causing them to be seen as either an embarrassment or a source of amusement to their peers.

- **Non-verbal communication**. There may be difficulties picking up cues from other people's body language and facial expressions and in modifying behaviour or actions accordingly.

- **Socially inappropriate language**. Sometimes irrelevant or inappropriate language can cause trouble or embarrassment. They can sometimes learn to use appropriate social communication skills in a given situation by direct instruction, but find it very difficult to spontaneously initiate or to generalise these.

- **Provocative language**. As teenagers, young people with ABI sometimes use language in such a way as to appear to be rude, inappropriate and challenging to authority.

Attention

A common everyday request for students in a learning environment is to pay attention, often with the assumption that this skill is within their automatic control. For most children and young people it is, but following even a mild ABI, there may be significant difficulties with the control of attentional processes, which can seriously compromise the ability to learn and lead to more generalised deficits in cognitive functioning (Catroppa and Anderson 2004). Problems with attention are among the most common cognitive problems associated with ABI. Also, those who experienced attentional difficulties prior to their injury often find that these are magnified.

What is sometimes thought to be a memory problem may, in fact, be due to a problem attending to the initial information. Attention and memory are cognitive processes that are closely interlinked. Attentional skills are also considered to be an important part of the executive system – the range of processes that are responsible for directing behaviour. Attentional problems may also be as a result of other issues, such as reduced hearing or vision. This underlines the complexity of the interrelationships between all aspects of functioning and the need for accurate assessment of perceived difficulties.

Attention is a broad term that refers to the skills necessary to receive and hold information in consciousness, e.g. thoughts, words, events, objects and input experienced by the senses. It includes a number of components and complex cognitive processes, which, during a normal course of child development, emerge at different ages and stages.

Components of attention

Arousal

Arousal is a term used in this context to denote alertness or the general state of readiness to respond to the environment and is necessary in order to attend and to make purposeful responses.

Sustained attention or vigilance

This is the ability to maintain attention over an extended period of time. It is often referred to as concentration or attention span and incorporates two elements: the ability to concentrate for an amount of time and the ability to maintain consistency of performance during that time. Sustained attention is disrupted if the student cannot continue to focus on a task at an age-appropriate level, even one that he is interested in, or can only focus on one that does not demand a response, such as watching a television programme.

Selective or focused attention

This is the aspect that people usually have in mind when talking about the notion of attention. It refers to the ability to filter out or to ignore distractions while focusing on an activity. A busy classroom has a multitude of potential distractors – a range of sounds, movements, sights, etc. – that can make it difficult for a student whose attentional mechanisms have been disrupted or damaged. He can easily be drawn off task by something irrelevant and, importantly, no longer has the control to bring his focus of attention back to what he is required to do. Conversely, students may also sometimes appear to be attentive, and environmental distractions can be minimal, but following ABI they are often more easily distracted by their own internal thoughts, which they have impaired ability to inhibit. Being hypersensitive to distractions makes working in classrooms where there are different activities going on simultaneously particularly hard for students after ABI; they have difficulties mentally blocking out what they can see and hear close by. They may often be described as being highly distractible.

Divided attention

Division of attention refers to the capacity to attend to more than one task, or to multiple components of a task at the same time – people may refer to this as 'multi-tasking'. A common example is the ability of many students to complete homework at the same time as listening to music or engaging with social media, or the ability to listen to teacher comments or instructions at the same time as continuing with another task. Being able to do more than one thing at once is often taken for granted because many of the everyday skills carried out simultaneously by most people are within their automatic repertoire, e.g. walking at the same time as talking, riding a bike at the same time as watching other traffic and reading road signs. Following an ABI, being able to carry out just one of them can 'use up' all of a young person's attentional capacity, so making it impossible for him to do two things at the same time. An important characteristic of attention is its limited capacity; only so much processing activity can take place at any time.

Shifting or alternating attention

This involves being able to flexibly change focus from one task to another, or from one dimension to another within a single task. Daily student life requires the need to change the focus of attention quickly and efficiently, from one activity to another within the same lesson, or from one subject to another. This is another particular aspect of attentional processing which many young people with ABI find hard to do. They appear to 'get stuck' on a train of thought and cannot easily make the transition to another topic. They can find it difficult to settle to a new task and may take longer to do so than their peers. If their attention is not focused at the start of a new task or topic, they may miss vital information. Changes to the timetable or routine at short notice can also be difficult for them to manage because a sudden change of plan requires a quick and effortless refocus of attention in a different direction.

Other relevant factors

In the normal course of child development, sustained attention matures relatively early, while processes for higher order or more complex skills, such as dividing or alternating attention, usually emerge later in childhood. Problems with these aspects of attention may, therefore, be one of the deficits that young people 'grow into' as they become older, e.g. older, teenage students may be expected to watch a video or listen to a classroom talk at the same time as taking notes, skills which would not be expected of younger children.

Various factors underlie impaired attention skills following ABI (Catroppa and Anderson 2004). The younger the age of the child at the time of injury, the more likely it is that the skills that are in the process of developing or have not yet developed will be impaired. This helps to explain why students may be able to successfully attend to some tasks but not others, depending on the demands and the nature of the attentional skills necessary for each.

Capacity to attend also depends on other factors, such as processing demands, motivation, levels of fatigue, etc. Almost all students, even those with marked attentional difficulties, can sustain attention in some situations. However, if an activity holds no interest for him, the young person needs to use more effort to concentrate, particularly if there are competing stimuli in which he is interested. What are commonly impaired following ABI are the internal controls to overcome this.

The kinds of strategies suitable for students with ADHD – Attention Deficit Hyperactivity Disorder – of a developmental nature may also be beneficial for those with acquired disorders. However, many students who have attentional deficits after ABI may also be hypo-active – i.e. they have slowed physical and mental agility.

Information processing

Information processing refers to the capacity of the brain for dealing with information and this is reflected in the efficiency, fluency and speed of response. There are two aspects: the speed of response to information, and the amount of information that can be processed at any time. There is a limit on both of these. Speed of processing information is closely linked to attentional skills, because the speed at which information is processed affects what can be noticed or 'taken in'. Any slowing down of the processes means that there is less capacity to attend.

Systems for processing information can easily become overloaded. This will, to a large extent, depend on the complexity of the information and the demands being made. The problems of processing overload often increase as the student progresses through his education and learning becomes more complex and more abstract. The student may be unable to follow lengthy or rapid instructions at a level expected for his age, and be slow to respond if he has speed of information processing deficits.

Learning and memory

Everything that we know and have learnt throughout our lives is stored in our memory. Without memory, we would not be able to use language; to recognise our friends and family; to read or to write; to learn how to cook or to drive a car; to choose what food to eat; or any other of the millions of activities that make up our daily lives. There are significant variations in different people's memory ability.

Acquired brain injury can disrupt memory to a significant and pervasive level, which bears no comparison with the minor difficulties that we all occasionally face when attempting to remember information.

Memory cannot be considered as a single function. To use the analogy of a library, information must be brought in, evaluated, categorised and stored. There must then be a system whereby any single piece of information can be accessed when required. It is also important that information can be cross-referenced. Use of a search engine on the Internet often produces a huge amount of information, almost instantly. Some of those same pieces of information would also be included, but as part of another set, if a different key word was entered. Our own brains are carrying out similar amazing feats all the time!

Different functions and areas of the brain are responsible for the many facets that combine to make up our memory ability. ABI may have affected some functions or areas more than others. It is, therefore, likely that a young person with ABI will have specific strengths and weaknesses with aspects of memory and in order to understand this, it is necessary to consider some of the different components of memory ability.

Memory processes

There are many different models of memory functioning but, as in the library analogy, most describe three main processes.

1 **Encoding.** This is the term used for 'taking in' information. This may be something that is read, heard, seen or experienced, which is then 'registered' in the brain. A person's ability to do this is closely linked with other factors, particularly attentional ability, which may also be affected following ABI.

2 **Storage.** This is a very complex process by which information is 'filed away' for future reference. There are different 'levels' of storage, for instance on a short- or long-term basis.

3 **Retrieval.** There is no conscious awareness of all the information that is filed away in our brains, so when this is needed, it must be retrieved from storage or transferred to consciousness. It may be possible to retrieve this deliberately – e.g. to remember a fact to answer a quiz question – or automatically – e.g. remembering how to drive without having to think about it. Information can be stored in our memories for a very long time, even throughout our lifetime. However, following an acquired brain injury, young people often cannot retrieve information over time, particularly if they have not practised recalling it soon after they have learnt it and then at subsequent intervals.

Theories of memory

The complexity of memory functions, and the ways in which we utilise or activate these for different purposes, can be described in different ways. However, theories of memory frequently refer to:

Working memory

The first 'holding point' for information that is registered in our brains is within what is often termed 'working memory'. This is information held in conscious memory at any one time. The capacity to hold information in this way is very limited, but can be increased slightly if the information is organised or grouped by meaning. Information is not automatically held in working memory, and we need to deliberately hold this there while it is sorted or organised. If a teacher gives a student instructions, these would normally initially be held in working memory.

Following an acquired brain injury, children and young people often have impairments of working memory. This may be related to the fact that they have not efficiently attended to the information in the first place, or that their organisational skills are poor and they cannot efficiently 'manipulate' or sort the information. If a student has difficulty with working memory, he can seem to ignore instructions or to be disorganised.

Episodic memory

This refers to memory for personal experiences or episodes in our lives. These events are not necessarily remembered consciously, but they are retained in memory. They can be termed 'autobiographical' memories: the who, what, when, where type of information. Young people with ABI may have difficulties remembering such events and experiences on an everyday basis.

Procedural memory

This refers to memory for actions or a 'procedure' that is learnt, usually through practise and repetition, which becomes automatic and which then does not have to be consciously considered. An example of this is the ability to drive a car. Once experienced, people do not consciously consider the learnt, 'mechanical' actions such as changing gear or turning the steering wheel. Young people with ABI often retain an ability to use this type of procedural memory relatively well.

Semantic memory

This refers to information and concepts which are explicitly learnt. This includes much academic learning – knowledge that is not acquired from personal experience. Many young people with ABI have significant difficulty deliberately learning semantic information out of context.

Explicit and implicit memory

Another way of classifying memory is in terms of deliberate or incidental learning – i.e. information that we make an effort to learn and that which we 'pick up' without realising it. Young children normally learn a great deal incidentally, through play and other experiences, and early years teachers are very aware of this.

- **Explicit memory** – conscious memories that can be verbalised (episodic or semantic memory)
- **Implicit memory** – memories of which we are not conscious (procedural memories or those relating to feelings or emotions)

It was thought that the formation of new explicit memories was the most likely to be affected by ABI, and while this is largely the case, some young people can show difficulties with both explicit and implicit memory, particularly if they sustained their brain injury at a very young age (Lah et al. 2011).

Sensory modalities

Memory can also be described in relation to the sensory modality with which it is initially encoded or 'registered'. Within the population in general, some people remember things that they have seen – **visual memory** – more readily than things that they hear – **auditory memory**. We are often consciously – or sub-consciously – aware of our own preferences, and some people, therefore, always like to write down verbal information that they need to remember. Others like to repeat something verbally if they are presented with it in writing. Use of our hands – for instance to write – can also help some people to remember, and this is referred to as **motor memory**; e.g. some people recall phone numbers by remembering the pattern of their fingers on the telephone key pad. Many students are encouraged to consider their preferred 'cognitive style' and then to utilise this to assist with their learning. Specific damage caused by ABI may affect a person's ability to remember information encoded via one of these methods. However, if the young person always preferred to remember information presented visually prior to his injury and this is now a relative weakness, it may be difficult for him to focus more on auditory information, even if this has then become a relative strength. It can be difficult to adapt one's 'cognitive style' to accommodate a different pattern of strengths and weaknesses.

Recall

The descriptions above relate to the ability to encode information, but there are also different ways by which this can be recalled. These processes can be impaired as a result of acquired brain injury. Our ability to recall or to retrieve information from our memory stores can be a deliberate process, involving a strategic search, or it can be an automatic process, whereby information is produced when required, e.g. vocabulary when speaking or writing. Prompts for deliberate recall are usually of the following types:

- **Free recall**. This is when a person is asked an open-ended question and has to search memory stores independently for the relevant information. Young people with memory impairments following ABI frequently find this very difficult – their retrieval skills are often disorganised and inefficient.

- **Cued recall**. This refers to instances where there is provision of a cue or prompt to help recall information from memory. This may, for instance, be in terms of a 'category' in which to search, or the initial sound of a word, etc. This often assists young people with memory impairments following ABI to retrieve stored information.

- **Recognition**. In this instance, the person is faced with a stimulus to which they can match information from memory. This type of recall is used in multiple-choice formats and is often a relative strength for young people with ABI.

Memory impairments

There are many contributory factors towards efficient memory. Information may not be efficiently encoded – or stored – but, equally, it may be stored but the person cannot retrieve it at all, or cannot do so quickly enough. If all the books in a library were tipped off the shelves and mixed up, it would take some considerable time to find specific information. However, some clues would help, such as the colour of the book's cover, hardback or paperback, large or small and so on.

Generally, lost memory ability cannot be restored – although there is often spontaneous recovery during the early stages after injury – but many strategies can be learnt to maximise ability and preserved strengths.

Perception

Perception relates to the way in which we process information that enters the body through one or more of our senses. All information that we receive from our environment must enter our brains via our vision, hearing, taste, touch or sense of smell.

The development of our ability to understand and to process information from our environment is incremental and increases as we store this from our experiences. Hence, once a young person has seen or heard certain things, knowledge regarding these will be stored and linked with future incoming information. Therefore, a young person who is familiar with such animals would be able to recognise a dog by touching it, even if he had his eyes shut, or by hearing it if he could not see it. As information regarding the sound, touch and appearance of a dog are linked in his memory store, he would also be able to tell you what sound it makes from just looking at it or what it feels like from just hearing it. The more that we experience, the more we are able to understand from sensory input and, with increasing developmental maturity, the more sophisticated our perceptual skills become. Therefore, memory is important to this development, as is language and organisation.

Increasingly, therefore, as children normally develop, perceptual ability becomes more closely linked with and inseparable from other cognitive skills.

As with all other areas of brain functioning, an acquired brain injury can disrupt aspects of perceptual processing. A not uncommon acquired impairment is a loss of ability to 'filter' incoming information and to focus on one aspect of this. Hence, young people who have suffered an acquired brain injury may find it difficult to cope with environments that are particularly noisy or which include high levels of sensory stimuli.

They may become hypersensitive to, for instance, noise or touch, e.g. someone rustling a newspaper, a cat purring or a minor itch. They may become unable to cope with or distinguish between more than one sensation concurrently, e.g. a bright visual display combined with sound. It is as if these incoming stimuli become confused so that the person soon reaches sensory 'overload'.

Visuo-perception

Visuo-perception is the ability to make sense of what is seen. This is not to be confused with vision, which is the ability to see. Impairment of visuo-perception is not uncommon following an acquired brain injury. It is also something that can easily be missed or misinterpreted, despite its potentially significant effects on academic progress and potential, including core skills of literacy and mathematics. There may be alteration to one or more aspects of visual perception, examples of which are given below.

Form constancy

This is the ability to recognise the actual shape of an object, symbol or figure, despite variations in the way that it is seen – e.g. a door that is closed, open or viewed from different parts of a room will look different, although the shape of the door itself will not change. The same shape can also be recognised despite being seen in different sizes, colours, etc. – e.g. a circle can be recognised when seen as a dinner plate, a letter 'O', a clock face or a window. If a student has impairment of this ability, it may affect many aspects of the curriculum involving visually presented material.

Figure ground perception

This is the ability to recognise shapes or objects as distinct from the background on which they are presented. If his desk is covered in books and papers, a student can usually look across it and pick out a visible item that he is looking for. Normally it is possible to 'filter out' other things within a field of vision and then focus on one specific thing. If a student has impairment of this ability, this may mean that he cannot search for things, cannot recognise one thing among others, or that he cannot play certain sports. It may also mean that he cannot read if there is too much information on the page or if the text is next to or over illustrations.

Position in space

This is the ability to recognise the orientation of an object or shape within 'space' – i.e. the immediate environment. If a young person sees a drawing on a page, he knows if it is upright or tilted at an angle and can usually tell if something has been placed upside down or back to front. If a student has impairment of this ability, he may be unaware of rotations and reversals. He may have difficulty matching identical shapes that are in a different orientation. This may affect his ability to efficiently recognise letters and numbers and to write these without reversals. It may affect his ability in practical subjects such as Technology or Science, as well as in Maths.

Spatial relations

This also refers to the ability to perceive shapes or objects within space but in relation to each other. It is important when deciding what can be fitted onto a page, or how close objects are to each other, or how fast something is moving. If a student has impairment of this ability, he may be unable to efficiently copy or create diagrams or illustrations; he may produce untidy work or lack understanding of where to place information on a page. He may start the top of a drawing at the bottom of a page and then wonder why he has run out of paper. He may have difficulty with some sports, bump into people or not seem aware of personal space, and he may be unsafe when crossing roads.

Visual closure

This is the ability to 'match' something that can only be seen partially – i.e. to 'visualise' the whole. From the relevant developmental stage, if a child saw the top of a chair – the rest being hidden under a table – he would still know what it was. If he saw a partially completed drawing of something familiar, he would know what it was. Students with impairment of these skills find it very difficult to visualise anything unless they can see the whole. This may affect their ability to draw conclusions from or to interpret any visually presented information, unless this is very explicit.

Executive functioning

Executive functioning is an umbrella term that refers to a range of skills needed to control and monitor all aspects of intentional behaviour. This describes almost all activities in daily home, learning and community settings; executive processes are required in order to succeed at any task that is non-routine. Cognitive processes, emotional responses and behavioural actions are all dependent on executive functioning. The term was so devised because it describes a collection of skills similar to those expected of an administrative executive – i.e. someone who makes plans, sets goals, organises ways in which those plans and goals can be achieved, and who is able to monitor and adjust the plans if necessary, apply sound judgement and have a good overall understanding and management of the situation.

There are a number of different regions of the brain that are involved in executive functioning processes, but the majority of these are subsumed within the frontal and prefrontal regions of the brain, which is why executive functioning deficits – or dysexecutive syndrome, as it is also called – have sometimes been referred to as 'frontal lobe difficulties', although the two are not synonymous. This area of the brain is very vulnerable to damage and so is commonly affected in acquired injury, often with very significant implications for a person's academic, social and emotional functioning.

Young people with ABI may, therefore, show difficulties with:

- **Planning and organising**. Because their thinking can be disorganised, it may be hard for them to identify and arrange the sequence of steps needed to carry out and complete a task – e.g. a student may dive in and start an activity without thinking about logical, sequential steps needed to succeed and then become very confused and frustrated when not knowing how to complete it.

- **Initiating and sustaining**. A student may have the knowledge and skills to carry out a task but be unable to get started – to initiate the activity – and to stick with it to completion, unless prompted by others. This can give others the impression that he is apathetic, unmotivated or unresponsive.

- **Goal setting**. This involves thinking about the 'end product' of a task or activity and working on something appropriate or relevant towards its completion. Without a goal in mind, thinking can be disjointed and disorganised – e.g. a young child may want to paint a picture – that, therefore, is his goal – so needs to be aware of the specific and sequential steps to be carried out to achieve it.

- **Inhibiting**. The student may be impulsive and unable to inhibit inappropriate language or behaviour. This can sometimes result in argumentative or aggressive responses to certain situations: he cannot easily stop and think about any implications of his actions or words before saying or doing them. He may make comments that are very hurtful. He can be overly affectionate with peers or staff, being unable to control the urge to make physical contact and unaware of the rules of social convention. There can be difficulties inhibiting attention to competing stimuli – e.g. in a busy classroom, a student's attention may be directed to activity or noise that is unrelated to the task in hand.

- **Problem solving** and making judgements. These are complex aspects of cognitive activity that are required when obstacles get in the way of achieving a goal. If a strategy does not work, the student with ABI may be completely unable to move forward and think of a different way to complete a task. Ylvisaker (1998) described the steps involved in organised deliberate problem solving as:

1 identifying the goal and clarifying the problem
2 gathering and considering information that may be relevant to solving the problem

3   exploring possible solutions, weighing their relative merits and choosing the best one
4   formulating a plan of action
5   executing the plan
6   monitoring and evaluating the plan's effectiveness.

Some problems have one correct solution but, as highlighted by Ylvisaker, most real-life problem solving is open-ended in that 'no rule or set of rules determines exactly what information is relevant in thinking about the problem or which of the possible solutions is best'.

Although this type of problem solving may sound as if it is only applicable to more complex tasks, young people must utilise this to complete all activities from the simplest to the most complex of everyday activities and for academic tasks ranging from a simple story to a post-graduate thesis! With the complex tasks, the process will be more of a conscious one, but we often plan, execute and amend more simple tasks without being particularly aware of that problem-solving process.

- **Self-monitoring**. This relates to difficulties with being able to gauge and evaluate the appropriateness of one's own behaviour. Young people with ABI may be oblivious to the reasons for getting into trouble and are unable to reflect on the implications of a course of action. They are often unable to benefit from feedback and so may continue to make the same mistakes. A lack of awareness of their deficits makes it hard to make adjustments.

- **Generalising newly acquired skills** to different settings. People with ABI can be very concrete in their thinking, which makes it hard for them to take information about what they have learnt and apply it in other situations.

- **Flexibility of thinking**. Difficulties may make it hard to cope with change – e.g. a sudden cancellation of an anticipated activity, a deviation from routine procedures, or an unfamiliar member of staff taking charge. Being able to adapt to new and variable situations is an integral part of problem solving.

- **Perseveration**. Students with ABI may 'get stuck' on a topic, idea, word or behaviour and repeat it, sometimes incessantly, oblivious to changes in the situation or conversation which make their actions or comments inappropriate.

Normal development and maturation of frontal brain regions emerges in infancy and continues throughout childhood into early adulthood. Development of executive function skills is closely aligned with this and skills develop rapidly throughout childhood. Some executive processes 'come on-line' at an earlier age than others. Key abilities subsumed by the frontal lobes are not, therefore, fully developed until late teens or early adult life. If damage to this area of the brain has affected the normal development of these skills, as may be the case following an ABI, this may not be fully apparent in a young child, with difficulties only gradually emerging years later.

It is important to remember that many of the difficulties identified above are normal at certain stages of childhood – e.g. inflexible thinking, lack of impulse control, verbal or physical aggressive outbursts and intolerance for delayed gratification are not unusual for a 2-year-old, but would be for a 12-year-old. This highlights the importance of making assessments in the context of a developmental framework.

The greatest difficulties are often not encountered until a student with ABI transfers from one setting to another, for instance from primary to secondary school. At secondary school, students are expected to be more independent, to take much greater responsibility for organising the equipment needed for each lesson, to quickly change from one set of tasks to another or from one room to another in a different part of the building, etc. What may be considered routine tasks, and effortlessly done by most students, can be overwhelming to students with executive functioning problems. For others, significant problems only emerge at the time of later transitions, for instance to college in late teenage years.

Impairments to executive functioning can mean that young people with otherwise good academic and intellectual ability can seem to lack 'common sense' and to have significant difficulties with social, behavioural, educational and everyday living skills.

Emma was in her late teens and had sustained an ABI as a younger child. With appropriate assistance she had done well at school, achieved qualifications and functioned well in her family home. She was being supported towards living independently and it was then that those working with her realised the everyday issues that she encountered. For instance, she had followed instructions to operate a washing machine efficiently, but when asked why she had only put one garment in this, she replied that the instructions on the garment were to 'wash coloured items separately'.

John, a young teenager who had sustained an ABI some years previously, attended a neuropsychological assessment while his parents waited elsewhere in the building. Following the assessment, in which he was shown to have overall well-preserved cognitive skills, he was asked what he would do if he went out to the waiting area and his parents were not there. He initially could think of nothing to do but then suggested some completely inappropriate courses of action.

Executive functioning deficits commonly manifest themselves in behaviour and social difficulties, which are described in more detail in Chapters 7 and 8. The executive system is an extremely complex one, and further useful information on its development during childhood has been detailed by Anderson (2002).

References

Anderson, P. (2002) 'Assessment and development of executive function during childhood'. *Child Neuropsychology* 8 (2), pp. 71–82.

Anderson, V., Northam, E., Hendy, J. and Wrennall, J. (2001) *Developmental Neuropsychology: A Clinical Approach.* Hove, East Sussex: Psychology Press.

Catroppa, C. and Anderson, V. (2004) 'Children's attentional skills 2 years post-traumatic brain injury'. *Journal of Developmental Neuropsychology* 23 (3), pp. 359–373.

Dick, F., Leech, R. and Richardson, F. (2008) 'The neuropsychology of language development', in Reed, J. and Warner-Rogers, J. (eds) *Child Neuropsychology.* Oxford: Wiley-Blackwell, pp. 139–182.

Duffy, J. R. (2012) *Motor Speech Disorders: Substrates, Differential Diagnosis, and Management.* London: Elsevier Mosby.

Gupta, Y. K. and Gupta, M. (2006) 'Post traumatic epilepsy: A review of scientific evidence'. *Indian Journal of Physiology and Pharmacology* 50 (1), pp. 7–16.

Lah, S., Epps, A., Levick, W. and Parry, L. (2011) 'Implicit and explicit memory outcome in children who have sustained severe traumatic brain injury: Impact of age at injury (preliminary findings)'. *Brain Injury* 25 (1), pp. 44–52.

Ouellet, M. C., Savard, J. and Morin, C. M. (2004) 'Insomnia following traumatic brain injury: A review'. *Neurorehabilitation and Neural Repair* 18 (4), pp. 187–198.

Powell, T. (1994) *Head Injury: A Practical Guide.* Nottingham: Headway National Head Injuries Association Ltd (2nd edition published 2001, Bicester: Winslow).

Sharp, N., Bye, R., Llewellyn, G. and Cusick, A. (2006) 'Fitting back in: Adolescents returning to school after severe acquired brain injury'. *Journal of Disability and Rehabilitation* 28 (12), pp. 767–778.

Ylvisaker, M. (ed) (1998) *Traumatic Brain Injury Rehabilitation: Children and Adolescents,* 2nd edn. Boston, MA: Butterworth-Heinemann.

Ylvisaker, M., Hartwick, P., Ross, B. and Nussbaum, N. (1994) 'Cognitive assessment', in Savage, R. and Wolcott, G. (eds) *Educational Dimensions of Acquired Brain Injury.* Austin, TX: Pro-Ed, pp. 69–120.

Planning school and college integration or reintegration

Successful re-entry requires a great deal of planning, which should begin once the school receives notice that a child has sustained a brain injury.

(Semrud-Clikeman 2001)

It is important to appreciate that rehabilitation following acquired brain injury in childhood is not only a brief service delivered in a medical setting, but a long-term, ongoing effort to help children and their families to achieve realistic goals in the child's everyday environments.

(Ylvisaker 1998)

The above quotations and the information below may be applicable to those with all severities of acquired brain injury: 'Teachers and parents need to be aware that improvement after mild/moderate traumatic brain injury varies dramatically and monitoring may need to occur throughout childhood and adolescence to avoid further problems and to ensure proper development' (Lloyd et al. 2015).

Rehabilitation can refer to the process of restoring skills and abilities that someone used to have but has lost due to illness or injury. This is in contrast to 'habilitation', which refers to assisting someone to acquire skills they have never had. For young people with acquired brain injury, it needs to be a combination of both. Although much reference is made to 'recovery', caution needs to be attached to its use; recovery suggests a return to the level of functioning and skills achieved prior to injury, which, in the case of brain injury, may not be achievable. Also, as childhood and adolescence marks a process of continuing development, re-acquiring previous levels of functioning may not be the ultimate goal.

Rehabilitation following acquired brain injury is a complex, enduring and often life-long process with the aim of maximising potential. It isn't just about the injured young person learning new skills. There is also an onus on others to prepare and adapt to changes resulting from the injury – such as those relating to the ability of the student to acquire new learning – and to understand the young person's needs. This can help to remove barriers to learning; the prevention of secondary problems; the provision of compensatory aids; and relevant modifications to the environment.

'Once a child returns to school following acquired brain injury, the educational system becomes the primary service provider for that child' (Ylvisaker et al. 1991). The opportunities that schools and colleges offer for structured learning programmes, close monitoring, regular and frequent support, and long-term planning make them very well placed to provide ongoing rehabilitation.

'School re-entry is usually an eagerly anticipated milestone along the child's recovery continuum. Too often, the dream becomes a nightmare' (Tucker and Colson 1992). Many parents and students, as well as members of staff, perceive the return to education as marking the return to normal life. The good physical recovery that most young people make, together with the recovery or retention of the surface features of language, can create an assumption that the return to education will be relatively smooth. It may be anticipated that any additional educational needs can be met by existing mainstream and special educational provision and practices. However, many students with acquired brain injury find the everyday tasks and expectations – the social, organisational and learning processes – that prior to their injury were well within their capabilities, to be subsequently problematic. The 'nightmare' referred to by Tucker and Colson above alludes to one or more of a range of potential issues, e.g. finding it hard to keep up with the pace of work; being misunderstood by education staff; having a rapidly diminishing group of friends; or being denied the degree of independence that peers enjoy.

Returning to school or college can be a very frightening experience for a young person who has had a moderate or severe ABI. He is often different; different from the person he once was, and different from his peers. He may have had little indication or understanding of those differences while away from the more usual education setting, particularly if any physical difficulties have resolved. These young people may have lost the comfortable familiarity of friends at school or college because of their lengthy absence; they may be returning to a different place of learning; they may have some signs of injury which set them apart from everyone else, and sooner or later after returning they may become frustrated, angry or confused when they are not able to do everyday activities that had previously been carried out effortlessly. Re-entering school/college confronts the young person with reality, and yet he may lack awareness of changes to his skill base. If failure is experienced, he may quickly lose self-confidence, become de-motivated and express his feelings in negative ways.

As considered in detail in Chapter 6, which relates to assessment, the nature and extent of any difficulties will depend on a variety of factors. This demands a highly individual approach to planning for re-entry based on each student's individual circumstances. However, there are key features common to successful educational reintegration that ideally should be considered as part of a core plan, some of which should be put into action at a very early stage of the young person's clinical treatment and continue into the educational setting (Savage and Wolcott 1995). These are set out below.

Joint planning for school or college re-entry

Preparation for successful school or college entry or re-entry involves careful planning and organisation well before full-time education is re-established. However, many young people currently re-enter school or college following an ABI without this benefit. Planning requires collaboration between all those involved in the student's health and educational welfare. In addition to family, school or college staff and relevant medical personnel, it may be useful or necessary to include advice from other professionals, such as the educational psychologist; an education administrator, if resources over and above those that the school can provide are required; specialist educational advisers, e.g. for visual impairment, behaviour or learning difficulties; a clinical psychologist; and therapists – each of whom brings a unique perspective and area of expertise. The relationship between them all, the quality of communication exchange, and a shared agreement of the role they can play will greatly influence the process and help to determine the ease with which the child or young person reintegrates. Studies suggest that many health and education professionals may lack knowledge and understanding about acquired brain injury (Linden et al. 2013; Linden and McClure 2012). It is therefore extremely important for all those involved that they be provided with detailed information about the young person's changed needs and the implications of acquired brain injuries for ongoing development and learning (see also pages 59–60 – In-service Training of Education Staff). Collaboration and proactive planning suggests a need for someone to co-ordinate and disseminate information overall, and so a named person should be identified to fulfil this role.

Ideally, initial contact between relevant personnel should take place as soon after the injury as possible. A plan for efficient and effective two-way flow of information needs to be established, as well as identification of the co-ordinator. If the young person is admitted to hospital with serious illness or injury, it is important for:

- the school/college to be informed as soon as possible
- a member of school/college staff to take responsibility for liaison with family and health personnel
- contact and visits to the injured young person to be encouraged when appropriate
- local authority special educational needs administrative section and educational psychology service to be notified if the student attends a maintained school (Although it may be unclear in the early stages after injury as to whether any advice or additional provision needs to be made, it can be helpful if the relevant services are informed about special circumstances as soon as possible.)
- discussions between relevant health and education representatives to be initiated

Working in partnership with parents

The Special Educational Needs and Disability Code of Practice in England emphasises the key role of the partnership between parents and professionals. Local authorities have a duty to make sure that young people and their parents are provided with information, advice and support to help them participate in discussions, planning and decision-making, not just about meeting educational needs but also in matters relating to health, social participation, increasing independence and preparation for adult life.

Parents know their child better than anyone else and may be the only ones who are aware of the extent of the changes that the brain injury has caused. However, making plans and decisions about any special educational arrangements can be a complicated and confusing process with which they may have had no previous experience. They may be asked to become involved in this process at the very time that they are already over-whelmed, still struggling to understand what has happened to their child, and juggling a host of other family and work commitments. The notion of parents being equal partners in planning and decision-making can sometimes be viewed sceptically by them. It is vital that members of health and education staff consider the emotional, financial and time pressures that parents may be under.

Educational planning can be a difficult and distressing issue for parents. Most parents envisage return to education as part of the continuing process of recovery towards pre-injury levels of academic achievement and social interaction. Their expectation may be that life will eventually be as it was before the injury, which is often reinforced if there appears to be good recovery of physical and language skills. It can be a lengthy and difficult procedure for them to understand and to accept that their child may require some special educational provision. They may also have to embark on a steep learning curve about special educational services and provision. In a very small number of cases, parents may be reluctant to become involved, or even be 'disengaged' from the process altogether. The impact of their child's acquired brain injury can be devastating for them and any lack of involvement may reflect overwhelming levels of stress or distress. There need to be equal measures of both sensitive support and understanding from staff working with parents (see Chapter 12).

Comprehensive assessment and identification of needs

Comprehensive multi-disciplinary assessment is an essential requirement for effective educational planning, and this needs to include information from the student's everyday settings as well as from standardised assessment. Identifying a young person's current strengths and needs will help to enable decisions about provision to be made prior to return. More detailed information about assessment is covered in Chapter 6.

Appropriate provision to meet needs

Provision refers to the ways in which needs are met and where they are met. The usual expectation is that students will return to the establishment that they were attending – or to the educational placement that was planned – prior to injury. However, for various reasons this may no longer be a viable option, e.g. the student's age, or requirements for specialist facilities. Many factors may need to be considered to identify the most appropriate educational setting, such as:

- physical access to buildings
- ongoing medical rehabilitation and provision of therapy – e.g. physiotherapy, speech and language therapy, occupational therapy
- access to technological equipment
- need for high level of structure
- staff expertise in a range of special educational needs – e.g. communication or sensory difficulties
- social, emotional and behavioural support.

'It would be highly desirable if one could end the dichotomy of "mainstream" and "special" schools which together provide a continuum of needs, with the local school as the first to be explored' (Connor 1997).

For the great majority of students with special educational needs, there is never any reason to consider provision other than at the local mainstream school. However, in England, if their needs are beyond the resources normally provided in the local school, an Education, Health and Care Plan may be required (see Chapter 9). Most students with Education, Health and Care Plans are educated in mainstream schools. For students with complex needs, it may be necessary to look at a wider range of options, including specialist provision.

Matching a student's needs to what a placement can offer may involve negotiation between parents or their advocates, the school or college, and key personnel in special education administration, particularly if additional resources are required. Parents, understandably, may prioritise what they perceive to be the best provision, even if that means requesting a school place out of their local area or in an independent school. A local authority priority is ensuring the most efficient use of financial resources for meeting the young person's needs. It is important that decisions about appropriate placement are primarily based on the needs of individual students and their family situations.

In-service training of education staff

Educators and parents are often unaware of the effects that ABI can have on a student's functioning, particularly in relation to cognitive skills and the impact on learning, behaviour and communication. They may be ill-prepared to address the needs of such students and to deal with the difficulties that are frequently faced. There may be little, if anything, in initial or in-service training of teachers and educational psychologists to alert them to the issues related to acquired brain injury that profoundly impact on students' ability to learn and to behave appropriately, issues that can be unique to this population. This lack of awareness is compounded by other professionals who, similarly, have not been made aware of long-term problems that young people can experience after acquired brain injury, and most especially when members of the medical profession declare that a good recovery – i.e. physical recovery – has been made.

It is therefore important that educators understand these needs to enable them to plan and provide an appropriate educational programme. Information should be provided which includes:

- what happens in a brain injury
- details of the particular young person's injury
- recovery patterns
- immediate and potential long-term effects of brain injury
- educational interventions that may be useful to consider.

The specific information about the student's injury should include the unique profile of needs, together with details of current strategies that have been successful.

Helping the young person, family and peers prepare for return to education

Any absence from education can disrupt peer relationships. Members of staff must take a lead in keeping the relationships alive. If the student is absent for a significant time, contact by letter, card, social media, email, phone or video as well as visits can help to sustain friendships and play an important part in maintaining a young person's morale.

Alistair sustained a severe brain injury in a road traffic accident and was in hospital for many months. At his primary school, there was reference to him every day in prayers at assembly and he was sent a weekly letter with contributions from different children. A video of his class was also prepared for him. His class teacher visited him regularly and brought one or two children from the class at each visit. The view of school staff was that they would continue to keep the memory of him alive until he returned.

A critical component of planning for return is the student's involvement, which needs to be appropriate to his age, level of understanding and skills. He should play as active a role as possible. He may benefit from help to become his own advocate and to be able to communicate his needs. Further information is provided about this in Chapter 6.

It is important to ensure that other students have factual information about the circumstances surrounding any injury – with the permission of the injured student or his parents/carers. Inaccurate information can be very damaging and upsetting, and information can become easily distorted, like Chinese whispers. In the case of a traumatic brain injury, other students may have witnessed the accident.

The informed involvement of other students increases the likelihood of a successful return. How this is dealt with must, if appropriate, first be discussed and agreed with the young person who is preparing to return and/or his parents. There must be respect for privacy and preferences when dealing with personal and sensitive details. However, some basic and simple information about the illness or injury can help peers and the student's siblings to make adjustments and accommodate possible changes in relationships. They often remark that their friend has changed, and even the most dedicated friends may eventually lose interest. It can be hard for them to understand how and why changes have occurred and they also need opportunities to express their feelings. Even if it is not possible to maintain or re-establish the kind of relationship they had prior to injury, the quality, warmth and sincerity can still be the same. However, it may require adult intervention and creative thinking to revitalise relationships.

Mohammed had been a popular and confident 15-year-old student. He suffered complications after the surgical removal of a brain tumour. He developed hydrocephalus and required the insertion of a shunt. He was also left with some mild cognitive and physical difficulties. He was anxious about how he looked and even more worried about how his peers at school would respond to him. He returned to school, initially on a part-time basis, and he prepared a short talk, which he wanted to present to his tutor group. He included information about what had happened to him and why he now had some physical problems, about the shunt that had been inserted, and what his rehabilitation programme consisted of. His form tutor was present and encouraged other students to ask Mohammed questions. Everyone was very pleased with how the session had gone and how useful it had been. Mohammed felt more confident about being back at school after having the topic brought out into the open. Other students showed a high degree of tolerance after being given the opportunity to talk and understand more about what had happened to Mohammed.

The injured student, too, may need much help to understand what has happened to him. This is a complex issue and many people who suffer an acquired brain injury have long-term significant difficulties with this understanding. A reduced level of self-awareness can be frustrating to family and friends, who comment that

> 'He doesn't think anything has changed.'
> 'He refuses to accept that he cannot do the kind of things he used to do.'

Limited self-awareness can also place the student at increased risk of further injury. Increasing awareness is often a complex issue, and one that has long been recognised as problematic following ABI. It is first of all important to increase the young person's knowledge of the events that have happened to him. The cognitive difficulties that may have resulted from the injury make it especially hard for the child or young person to understand, so the task of 'filling in the gaps' and rectifying any misunderstandings or inaccurate knowledge must be delivered in a sensitive way. Compiling an 'autobiography', or life story, starting from the student's very early life, that is age appropriate in its content and presentation, can be very helpful. It also helps to put the illness or injury in a chronological context, which, in years to come, may be helpful for the young person with memory difficulties. This could be a gradually evolving project, carried out on a regular and frequent basis using much pictorial information. Presentation in a ring binder allows the student to share any of his contributions to his story, while ensuring that other parts remain private, in what can be a very personal account. Some parents initially find it difficult to go over the events with their child because of their own emotional involvement, but have found it easier to then talk about them in the context of this life story. Indeed, they have sometimes benefited themselves from this compilation of events that their child has put together with help, perhaps, from a counsellor or a personal tutor.

The type of information regarding the injury that is included will obviously be related to the student's unique circumstances and family history, but the following list may serve as a useful guide when helping a child or young person to understand the facts and sequences (developed from Beardmore et al. 1999):

Story of the accident or illness

- Orientation: When the injury or illness occurred – how long ago?
- Story of the accident or illness: Where was it? What happened?

Hospitalisation

- Name of hospital/s
- Length of time in hospital
- Knowledge of hospital procedures or operations

Brain injury

- Understanding of the term
- Knowledge of brain functioning – appropriate to age or developmental stage
- Knowledge of what happened to the brain when it was injured

Coma

- Correct description of coma
- Duration of coma

Long-term effects of brain injury

- Common problems occurring afterwards
- Knowledge of personal deficits, difficulties or disabilities

Time at home or in rehabilitation before return to education

- Progress and activities

Interventions to help increase a young person's understanding and awareness of their brain injury and what has happened to them is an important part of their rehabilitation. Addressing issues involving trauma, loss, change, identity and insight require high levels of sensitive support. Details of a narrative approach to help with these, specifically used with young people with acquired brain injury, have been described by Perkins (2015). Additional resources may also be found in life story work and related books, e.g. Camis (2001) *My Life and Me*; Ryan and Walker (2016) *Life Story Work: Why, What, How and When*; and Hammond and Cooper (2013) *Digital Life Story Work*. These include a range of techniques and suggested digital technologies to provide interactive and practical activities for helping young people understand changes in their lives. Approaches to life story work were originally designed by social workers for helping young people in the fostering or adoption process. However, many of the approaches may be useful for those supporting young people with ABI.

Review and follow-up

The need for ongoing communication between health, education and family personnel after a young person has been discharged from the hospital or rehabilitation facility cannot be overstated. After returning home, families can feel isolated and scared. There may be no one in their home area who understands their anxieties and, rather than ame-liorating with time, they often increase. The return home can also be the very time when the expertise of the medical staff is most required, ensuring that an effective handover to local or community counterparts has been undertaken, medical advice has been acknowledged and understood, and liaison with education staff continues.

Special consideration of preschool children

The impact of an acquired brain injury to a very young child can be devastating. Immature brains are very vulnerable to injury at a crucial time during their development. The younger the child, the fewer the skills that have already been learnt and established. Generally, new learning is more problematic after an ABI than retrieval of previously learnt skills, and therefore young children are at much greater risk for delayed or maladaptive learning than older children because of their more limited knowledge base. There needs to be heightened awareness of the possibility of 'growing into' disability for children who have not yet reached an age at which particular skills are expected to emerge (Anderson et al. 2011).

A child who is below statutory school age may or may not be attending an early years setting. However, whatever the arrangements for preschool provision, it is important that the local authority is made aware of any special needs that have resulted from a child's ABI, and that there is provision during the early years as well as careful planning and preparation for the time when the child enters school.

Entering school for the first time with an injured brain can create additional stress factors. It is crucial that members of school staff pay very close attention to the child's learning and behavioural responses and have an awareness of the possible consequences of injury. It is also important to acknowledge the enormous variation of skills and behaviours that can normally be demonstrated by very young children, and to be cautious about over-interpreting. However, early intervention is critical for minimising the negative effects of acquired injury.

Summary

Key points for discussion and action to help ensure successful re-entry to education that should be instigated prior to return should include:

- identification of student's current strengths and needs
- staff training about student's brain injury issues
- return or start date at educational placement
- plans for phased re-entry; determine extent of any part-time attendance
- length of day
- plans for social integration and peer support
- identification of key staff member or personal tutor for liaison and monitoring of student's progress

- arrangements for rest or less cognitively challenging times
- selection of curricular activities best suited to the student's needs and interests and expectations of participation
- student's timetable and any additional resources or facilities
- management of unstructured time
- access to different areas of building – e.g. can stairs be negotiated?
- homework policy
- communication and reporting systems between home and educational facility
- communication and reporting systems between education and health personnel
- transport or travel arrangements
- date of first review.

References

Anderson, V., Spencer-Smith, M. and Wood, A. (2011) 'Do children really recover better? Neurobehavioural plasticity after early brain insult'. *Brain* 134, pp. 2197–2221.

Beardmore, S., Tate, R. and Liddle, B. (1999) 'Does information and feedback improve children's knowledge and awareness of deficits after traumatic brain injury?'. *Neuropsychological Rehabilitation* 9 (1), pp. 45–62.

Camis, J. (2001) *My Life and Me*. London: British Association for Adoption & Fostering.

Connor, M. (1997) 'Parental motivation for specialist or mainstream placement'. *Support for Learning* 12 (3), pp. 104–110.

Hammond, S. and Cooper, N. (2013) *Digital Life Story Work*. London: British Association of Adoption & Fostering (now CoramBAAF Adoption and Fostering Academy).

Linden, M. A., Braiden, H. J. and Miller, S. (2013) 'Education professionals' understanding of childhood traumatic brain injury'. *Brain Injury* 27 (1), pp. 92–102.

Linden, M. A. and McClure, J. (2012) 'The causal attributions of nursing students towards adolescent survivors of brain injury'. *Nursing Research* 61 (1), pp. 58–65.

Lloyd, J., Wilson, M. L., Tenovou, O. and Saarijarvi, S. (2015) 'Outcomes from mild and moderate traumatic brain injuries among children and adolescents: A systematic review of studies from 2008–2013'. *Brain Injury* 29 (5), pp. 539–549.

Perkins, A. (2015) 'Psychological support using narrative psychotherapy for children with brain injury', in Reed, J., Byard, K. and Fine, H. (eds) *Neuropsychological Rehabilitation of Childhood Brain Injury: A Practical Guide*. Basingstoke: Palgrave Macmillan, pp. 215–234.

Ryan, T. and Walker, R. (2016) *Life Story Work: Why, What, How and When*. London: CoramBAAF.

Savage, R. C. and Wolcott, G. F. (1995) *An Educator's Manual: What Educators Need to Know about Students with Brain Injury*. Washington, DC: Brain Injury Association Inc.

Semrud-Clikeman, M. (2001) *Traumatic Brain Injury in Children and Adolescents: Assessment and Intervention.* New York: Guilford.

Tucker, B. F. and Colson, S. E. (1992) 'Traumatic brain injury: An overview of school reentry'. *Intervention in School and Clinic* 27 (4), pp. 198–206.

Ylvisaker, M. (ed) (1998) *Traumatic Brain Injury Rehabilitation: Children and Adolescents,* 2nd edn. Boston, MA: Butterworth-Heinemann.

Ylvisaker, M., Hartwick, P. and Stevens, M. (1991) 'School re-entry following head injury: Managing the transition from hospital to school'. *Journal of Head Trauma Rehabilitation* 6 (1), pp. 10–22.

Assessment of children and young people with ABI

We recommend that underlying cognitive processes are comprehensively assessed and considered in the context of cognitive development, and the individual's wider psychosocial needs and environment, to generate an appropriately individualized intervention programme.

(Limond and Adlam 2015)

Cognitive Assessment

Assessment is an essential component of the planning for entering or returning to school or college after an acquired brain injury. There may be significant cognitive, sensory, self-regulatory and other behavioural changes resulting from the brain injury which can have profound effects on a young person's ability to learn and socialise. A broad-based assessment is required to identify these.

Many students return to school after an ABI without having a cognitive assessment, and indeed, for those with a mild injury, this may not be required if close monitoring indicates no changes from prior to injury. However, it is important that young people who do experience substantial changes in learning or behaviour be referred for a psychological assessment. This chapter is not about how to assess, or which specific tools to consider using, but is to emphasise the significant factors that may need to be taken into account when planning and carrying out assessment of young people with ABI.

An essential factor in any assessment of a young person with ABI is the knowledge and experience of the psychologist undertaking that assessment. This needs to include:

- **Sound understanding of normal child and adolescent development**, how and when skills usually emerge and how interruption to development can impact on different cognitive processes at different ages and stages of the development. For example, some behaviours or difficulties commonly associated with ABI and observed or notably absent in a child, particularly a young one, may not be significant or unusual at all in a developmental context.

- **Understanding and experience of paediatric neuropsychology and assessment procedures.** It is well recognised that many cognitive impairments following acquired brain injury are not detected by clinical neurological examination, nor solely by commonly used standardised measures of intelligence, and that these are more likely to be identified by neuropsychological assessment. Neuropsychological assessment is used to help understand the impact that injury to the brain, and the physiological make-up of the brain, may have on cognitive functioning. This is sometimes referred to as brain-behaviour relationships. An assessment may involve a variety of tests designed to evaluate a range of functions such as memory, speed of processing information, reasoning, problem solving, and language functions (see page 74 for more details of what may need to be assessed).

  Middleton (2000) emphasises the dangers of using adult models of neuropsychology and assessment tools originally devised for adults. An injury to a developing brain may be qualitatively different to a similar kind of injury in a fully mature adult brain, and so extrapolating information from adult tests or populations and applying it to children and young people may be unsuitable and lack appropriate normative information. Also, tests designed for adults may be of little interest to young children, and do nothing to capture their attention.

- **Understanding of contextual and wider environmental factors** which play a key role in the young person's functioning. It is therefore critical to appreciate the influence of these in any kind of assessment (see page 78).

- **Familiarity with education systems and sharing of information.** A psychological assessment has very limited value unless it includes information about the implications and recommendations for the educational and social environment. It has even less value if that information is not conveyed to the key individuals responsible for the student's learning. The assessment report needs to include an interpretation of test results and other information gathered, using language that can be readily understood by education staff, with practical suggestions and strategies that can be implemented within the context of the learning environment.

Information from the assessment is required in order to help:

- understand changes in learning and behaviour
- identify how the student learns and uses new information
- develop educational goals and plans
- devise compensatory strategies and evaluate their efficacy
- provide a baseline of cognitive and behavioural strengths and difficulties
- document improvements or changes in functioning
- understand how social, motivational and environmental factors affect performance
- provide evidence of the need for additional or different supports.

Assessment principles

Multi-disciplinary information

There is no single approach, individual or discipline that can evaluate the spectrum of needs after an acquired brain injury. The factors affecting learning, behaviour and social deficits after an ABI are interrelated, often complex and diverse, and can affect any or many areas of functioning, which cross the boundaries of a number of disciplines and situations. Specific aspects of functioning cannot be assessed and supported in isolation from others. The emphasis must be on the interrelationship between factors involved rather than any of the individual measures or on hypotheses based on areas of the brain which have been damaged.

Information from a variety of settings and from a range of people who bring their different knowledge, perspectives and experience is therefore required in order to understand the full impact of the brain injury and the underlying causes of a young person's difficulties, and to formulate recommendations. The uniqueness and diversity of difficulties experienced following ABI precludes a set procedure for assessment.

The overriding issue is the importance of collaboration and a framework which is shared by all involved in any evaluation. Without this, there is a danger of over-assessment – different disciplines or professionals using similar tests, or sometimes even the same ones, to assess the same areas of functioning – or under-assessment – with some areas of functioning being ignored. There can often be considerable overlap of professional areas of interest and it is unacceptable to carry out more intrusive assessment procedures than necessary, as well as risking invalidating results due to repetition of the same assessment measures within a short space of time.

It is essential to be aware of the professionals that have been or are currently involved in addition to education staff. These could include any combination of speech and language therapist, occupational therapist, physiotherapist, community paediatrician, neurologist, psychiatrist, social worker, hospital teacher, or clinical and/or educational psychologist. This list is by no means exclusive and parents may be best placed to identify who has had contact with their child.

Clinical assessments of physical, sensory and language skills of young people with ABI can provide essential information that contributes to an assessment of cognitive functioning. These are outside the scope of this book, but details can be found in Ylvisaker (1998), Blosser and DePompei (2003) and Hooper (2013).

Planning for assessment

This should include knowledge of:

- what it is that needs to be assessed
- the sources from which the information is to be obtained
- the assessment approaches and tools, including appropriate modes of communication.

Assessment may need to be a combination of: information about pre-injury functioning in education, social and home environments; perceptions and observations of those who work closely with the young person; observation of current functioning in a range of settings; and norm-referenced and dynamic assessment.

Comparing pre-injury performance and skills with current ones

This helps to identify and explain the extent and nature of the unique cognitive, physical and behavioural changes. Functioning prior to injury – skills, achievements, needs, personality, preferences, record of attendance, etc. – can still have an impact after injury and this is important to know when identifying relevant and realistic goals for change. If difficulties were experienced in a particular area of functioning before the injury, it is highly likely that these will continue to be apparent, and may be even more problematic.

Parental contribution

This is a vital part of the process. Parents know their son or daughter better than anyone else and they can provide insights into important aspects of earlier and current functioning that is difficult to glean from anyone else, e.g. relationships with siblings, the young person's ability to function in the home and in community settings, and the level and extent of social contacts and activities.

It can be very useful if parents are able to provide information about their child's growth and development, with details of birth, infancy and early childhood, previous medical history, social/emotional development and progress at nursery and school. The following checklist may be helpful:

Pre-injury progress

- Developmental milestones and health history
- Progress at nursery and school
- Any need for additional help in school – e.g. with reading
- Any behavioural or emotional difficulties
- Any physical or sensory – sight, hearing, etc. – difficulties
- Interests/hobbies during leisure time
- Personality – e.g. quiet or extrovert, shy or confident
- Relationships with family members and friends

Details of the illness or accident

- The trauma; what happened and when
- The range of functions the injury has affected – e.g. orthopaedic or other injuries

- Length of stay in hospital
- Any formal rehabilitation – inpatient/outpatient – the young person has received and the therapists that were/are involved

Changes and current functioning in

- Mobility skills – e.g. walking, running, climbing
- Self-help skills – e.g. eating, drinking, dressing, toileting, etc. Is any help needed, and if so, how much?
- Sensory skills – vision, hearing, taste, smell, touch
- Conversation – use of words, clarity of speech, speed of talking and responding
- Memory skills – e.g. any difficulties remembering information and any particular strategies that help at home, such as making lists or keeping a diary?
- Attention skills – any specific strategies at home that help with concentration?
- Energy levels, rest and sleep – e.g. does he get more tired now and is this at particular times of the day/week? Are there any changes to sleep routines?
- Speed of doing tasks – e.g. does it now take him any longer to get things done?
- Behaviour – e.g. any tantrums, anger or aggression, impulsivity, inappropriate behaviour or speech? Any concerns with sexual behaviour?
- Mood and personality – e.g. is he quieter or more withdrawn?
- Friendships and social life – e.g. does the young person initiate social contact with others of similar age, maintain friendships from prior to the injury or spend much time alone?
- Leisure time activities and how his time out of school or college is spent? – e.g. hobbies, interests, etc. Can he play or organise his time constructively when alone?
- Independence – e.g. in what ways is he now more reliant on others? Are there any safety issues as a result of the injury?

Parental views about progress at school/college

- Areas in which success is experienced
- Current difficulties
- Ability to concentrate and to finish tasks
- Changes in reading, writing and spelling skills
- Changes in ability to remember, organise, plan, problem solve and reason
- Successful approaches that help with learning – e.g. extra adult support or strategies
- Ability to manage changing classes or teachers, and unexpected changes to the routine

- Any difficulties at break or lunchtimes?

- If homework is expected, are there any particular issues with it – e.g. can he organise and complete it independently? Is much assistance required and given?

- Does he like school/college and want to go?

- Is he reasonably organised – for his age – with books and equipment, clothes, jobs at home, etc.?

- To what extent is he aware of any learning, behaviour or social changes?

Parental views about additional needs in school/college

- What, if any, are the young person's special educational needs considered to be?

- Are they being well met? If not, what is required?

- Do they have any concerns regarding present and future education?

- What are the most important rehabilitation/educational goals?

Effects on the whole family

- Effects that the young person's illness or injury has had on the family as a whole and the relationships within it.

Young person's contribution to assessment

The importance of listening to the views of young people together with their active participation in assessment and decision-making that affects their lives is now widely accepted. Local authorities have a duty to make sure that those with special needs, and their parents, are provided with the information, advice and support to enable them to do so. This may be with a view to setting learning targets, contributing to reviews and assessments, transition planning, indicating preferences, or discussion about choice of school or college, etc.

Young people may need much encouragement and support to be actively involved and acknowledge or be aware of their current strengths and difficulties. This can sometimes be a particularly challenging issue given the cognitive and communication deficits that may be experienced. However, a lack of awareness of deficits or difficulties in communication should in no way preclude involvement and there are many ways in which decisions can be made with rather than for a young person. Education staff may need to learn how to actively encourage the young person, especially if there are communication difficulties. Communication passports – person-centred booklets for those who cannot easily speak for themselves – may be helpful. These can provide information about the most effective means of communicating, and about a young person's views and preferences. Augmentative and alternative communication aids and advice from a speech and language therapist may be helpful. Interactive resources using picture communication symbols may be useful tools for those with relevant training in their use, e.g. 'Talking Mats' Aitken and Millar (2000), if reliance on spoken language is inappropriate.

Blosser and DePompei (2003) provide pertinent questions – adapted below – that can be asked of young people who have returned to education after an injury. These can be used and adapted in a discussion or written format, depending on a student's capabilities:

1   What problems are you experiencing in class? What are the problems that you are having since you returned to school/college?

2   How do you usually act when you are experiencing problems or frustrations in class? List some of the ways you behave when you are having problems.

3   What classroom situation causes you the most problems?
   a) Noise
   b) Temperature
   c) Pictures and wall decorations
   d) Other people in the room
   e) Other things

4   What are the ways people – your teachers/assistants/classmates – help you when you experience trouble in class?

5   What do you think people should do to help you?

6   What things do people do to frustrate you or cause you more problems?

7   What do you think people should **stop** doing when they are around you?

8   At what time of day do you do your best?
   a) Early morning
   b) Mid-morning
   c) Around the middle of the day
   d) Mid-afternoon
   e) Early evening
   f) Late evening

Why do you think this is your best time of day?

9   If you could choose three skills to improve, what would they be?

10 What are five things that are great about you that you would like other people to know?

Areas that may be evaluated in a neuropsychological assessment

General intellectual ability

- Verbal
- Non-verbal

Attention/concentration

- Visual
- Auditory

Language and communication

- Expressive language
- Receptive language
- Written language

Memory and learning

- Visual/Auditory
- Immediate/Delayed
- Recall/Recognition

Perception

- Visual
- Visual/Motor
- Auditory
- Sensory

Speed of information processing

- Motor speed
- Thinking speed

Executive skills

- Planning and organising
- Initiating
- Goal setting
- Inhibiting
- Problem solving
- Self-monitoring
- Flexibility of thought

Orientation

- Time
- Place
- Person

Educational attainments

- Reading – accuracy, comprehension, fluency, speed
- Spelling
- Recording – handwriting, word-processing
- Maths – arithmetic, reasoning

Personality: adjustment and behaviour at school/college and home

- Social skills
- Self-concept
- Behavioural control
- Frustration tolerance

Additional considerations that may impact on assessment of cognitive functioning

- Stamina and fatigue
- School/college attendance
- Consistency of performance
- Insight/awareness
- Health/medical conditions
- Effects of medication
- Interests and preferences
- Attitudes and fears
- Cultural factors
- First/foreign language factors

Limitations of standardised assessment

Standardised assessments are tests that are administered and scored according to pre-determined 'standard' procedures. They are carried out in the same way with everyone who they are given to. Standardised measures can be useful for assessing a wide range of skills that may be affected by ABI. They also enable comparison of a student's performance with that of others of the same age and provide a measure of change over time, indicating if there has been deterioration or gains in performance.

An understanding of the unique issues of ABI includes an appreciation that test scores can overestimate a student's ability in the classroom and other real-life situations. Most assessments provide estimates of optimal rather than typical levels of functioning. Results may be misleading and there is a danger of false optimism if the following are not taken into account:

- Scores may reflect a good recovery of skills learnt prior to the ABI rather than current learning abilities.

- Attention deficits in a busy classroom may not be obvious in a quiet assessment setting that offers one-to-one interaction.

- Decreased endurance or persistence may not be apparent if the presented tasks are short and novel.

- Impaired initiation, planning and organisation skills may not be observable in a highly structured setting with provision of precise, unambiguous instructions and when the criteria for success are clearly specified.

- Memory and information-processing demands within the duration of an assessment session may not be the same as those involved in the carry-over of information from lesson to lesson or week to week, as is expected in a typical education setting.

- A one-off assessment session does not make allowances for frequent inconsistencies in performance that can be experienced following ABI.

- Continued change and recovery of lost or impaired skills can restrict the usefulness of test results.

(Adapted from Ylvisaker et al. 1994)

Intelligence testing

Traditional IQ tests 'tap' what has already been learnt and therefore do not usually reflect significant deficits after brain injury. Even students who have had a moderate to severe injury, which results in significant learning difficulties, may score within the normal range on a standardised intelligence test. Measurements of verbal IQ can sometimes provide an estimate of pre-injury status because skills acquired prior to injury may be preserved or recovered relatively quickly. Measurements of 'performance' IQ require physical manipulation of objects. They may provide a better measure of loss and improvement because visuo-perceptual and visuo-motor skills are not so easily recovered, and the ability to learn new skills, solve problems and work at speed is most commonly affected.

Dynamic assessment

This offers an approach that is an alternative, or a supplement, to normative testing measures and the principles lend themselves very well to working with children and young people with ABI (Ylvisaker and Gioia 1998). Dynamic assessment focuses on a student's ability to learn, and not on what has already been learnt. In conventional testing situations, the examiner presents items to a young person and records the response without any attempt to intervene in order to guide, or improve, his performance. Information from traditional 'static' tests are a snapshot and do not necessarily provide any indication of a student's potential for change. Dynamic assessment aims to evaluate the ability of the young person to learn from interaction with a teacher, through observation of his responsiveness to instruction and guidance on particular tasks. The strategies used in dynamic assessment are more closely related to the kind of learning processes that already take place in real-life educational environments – e.g. the teacher asks leading questions, demonstrates, starts to solve a task and asks the student to continue. The ability to learn is based on the premise that a young person's knowledge develops during interactions with more capable others. Acquisition of new learning initially requires maximum assistance from an adult but gradually the student develops greater responsibility for the activity/learning task as the information becomes internalised. The aim of the assessment process is to evaluate the amount of change that can occur during the interactions with the examiner, the focus being not so much on *what* a young person learns but more on *how much* and *what kinds of information and guidance* are required in order for learning to occur. Dynamic assessment has been reported to provide 'down to earth and usable advice for teachers and special needs assistants as a direct result of assessment' (Deutsch and Reynolds 2000). There is considerable interest in the use of this assessment approach, and it is becoming more widely practised by psychologists and endorsed by the UK government's support for the teaching of thinking skills. Further information about dynamic assessment can be found in Birnbaum and Deutsch (1996), Sternberg and Grigorenko (2002), and Haywood and Lidz (2007).

Functional assessment

There may well be significant benefit in carrying out some individual assessment tasks which require the assessor and student to work away from the classroom in a distraction-free area, but much information that is useful needs to be gathered from functional settings and from those who work in them with the student. It is important to be aware that skills learnt or demonstrated in isolation from everyday situations in which they would be typically used may be harder to put into practice in 'real life'. In real life, skills frequently need to be applied flexibly with an ability to problem-solve and respond in a range of scenarios. Assessment of a young person's ability to do so would typically be obtained using a range of methods from observation, interviews with education staff and/or parents, questionnaires or inventories, records of the student's work, curriculum information, etc. Obviously the younger the child, the more limited the availability of educational information. Contact with a preschool child's community service providers, e.g. Health Visitor or playgroup/nursery staff, may therefore be helpful.

Assessment of contextual/environmental factors

Although the focus of an assessment is the young person, he does not exist in isolation and must be considered in relation to his environment. The importance of ongoing contextualised assessment cannot be overstated. Factors in home, education or community life in which the student may be experiencing difficulties must be taken into account. Young people interact with education staff, family, friends, peers, etc., all of whom will influence learning and social behaviours, to a lesser or greater extent.

It is also important to remember that, as indicated above, a young person's abilities in the kind of atypical setting that usually occurs when standardised normative assessment is carried out – e.g. a one-to-one, relatively distraction-free, highly structured situation – can lead to overestimates of actual abilities in the classroom. Within a busy classroom, during a normal day, a student's ability to attend, plan, organise and problem-solve will be taxed to a much greater extent. What is just as important as assessing skills or knowledge is how or whether the young person is able to use that knowledge. Young people with ABI may have theoretical knowledge but be unable to apply that to functional situations.

Many factors within the education setting, listed below, may have considerable impact on a student's ability to learn and to behave appropriately and, therefore, need to be considered when assessing and making recommendations.

Environmental factors

- Ethos of learning establishment and management style
- Class size

- Acknowledgement of needs
- Behaviour policy
- Current ways of supporting any difficulties
- Consistency of staff
- Cues or prompts

- Length of concentrated learning periods
- Seating position and arrangements
- Peer models
- Classroom space
- Peer support

- Reinforcement frequency
- Degree of structure

78

- Activity level
- Routines
- Noise

- Lighting

- Temperature

- Availability of choice
- Classroom organisation
- Playground/leisure time management
- Management of dining arrangements
- Transitions – transferring from class to class

Instructional factors

- Task level and clarity
- Task adaptations/differentiation
- Expectations/differentiation
- Time restrictions
- Opportunities for success
- Equipment
- Task performance
- Auditory demands
- Task familiarity
- Attentional demands
- Visual demands
- Memory demands
- Task interest

- Task length
- Homework demands
- Verbal reinforcement
- Pace of delivering
- Recapping of previous learning
- Opportunities for rehearsal/practice
- Changes in activity
- Reading demands
- Frequency of feedback
- Teaching style and mode of instruction
- Teacher and other adult support
- Advance organisers
- Task format

Reporting assessment information

A written report is usually the most enduring part of an assessment and can be the most effective way of recording and conveying information gathered during the process. However, there needs to be awareness that it can also be the least efficient way of communicating information if the report fails to be seen by those in a position to implement recommendations. Reports can easily be filed away without the advice in them being brought to the notice of staff who work directly with the student. It is important that the person who conducted the assessment makes direct contact with the parents and the relevant member of staff in the school or college to discuss the implications of the written report. This ensures that the most pertinent information reaches them, and also the personal contact can encourage the staff to take greater interest in the issues and responsibility for the implementation of the recommendations.

Assessment after an acquired brain injury very often focuses on loss, particularly on the areas of functioning with which the young person currently has difficulties. It is important to acknowledge positive aspects by including information about a student's strengths, abilities and interests.

Feedback to the young person who has participated in any kind of assessment is important. This can usually be done using clear, simple language and/or symbols that are meaningful and appropriate, explaining strengths and needs honestly with examples and analogies. It is vital that the young person is not overwhelmed and is helped to see any problems that are described as manageable. He needs to be an integral part of any process of change. Not only do children and young people have an important right to participate in decisions and issues that affect them, but discussion, negotiation and agreement of simple structured objectives can increase the likelihood for success of any plans to be put into effect.

Statutory assessment (England)

All local authorities are required to make provision for children and young people with special educational needs. This is usually funded and provided by the budget of the nursery, school or college that the young person attends. Some children and young people may require a level or kind of provision that costs more than can be provided by that budget. This may involve a more formal wider assessment of their educational, health and care needs. It is sometimes referred to as a statutory assessment because the local authority is required to carry it out under the statute of the Children and Families Act 2014. It is applicable to young people up to the age of 25. The assessment may lead to the production of an Education, Health and Care Plan (see Chapter 9 on Individual Education Planning).

Periodic and ongoing evaluation

Assessment following ABI must be viewed as an ongoing process. Assessment may have been carried out while the young person was attending a hospital or rehabilitation centre as either an inpatient or outpatient. This information is useful for helping to determine the needs and kinds of support to be put into place for return to school or college. However, there will be additional and important information as the student adapts to the environment. After a period of settling in and orientating to the longer-term setting, it is essential to assess how cognitive and functional impairments impact on a young person's ability to successfully integrate socially and academically, i.e. his learning and behaviour in more usual environments. It is also easier for the student to be actively involved in the process of assessment and review when back in a familiar environment.

Because of the nature of recovery or ongoing development after ABI, assessments need to be undertaken more often than is normally the case with other young people. Those with ABI may have a more frequently changing profile of skills and needs than their peers and some information can quickly become outdated. They may demonstrate rapid improvements in some skill areas and make very limited gains in others. Some problems may not be evident until years after injury, making ongoing monitoring essential in order to appreciate the extent of any resulting developmental difficulties.

Commonly, there is a cumulative effect of the damage on the rate of development, and so there is often a widening of the gap in relation to peers over time. This means that the learning challenges increase for young people with ABI as they progress through educational stages. Informal monitoring and appraisal should be ongoing within education, and this is an important source of information for determining the appropriate level of tasks and support. Curriculum information contributes to this too and helps to make comparisons with other students at the same stage, which parents in particular find useful for gauging how their child is progressing. A very frequent parental question is: How is my child doing compared to everyone else in the class? Reassessment using psychometric measures – a way of assessing a person's skills, or ability, or aspects of personality in a structured, standardised way that enables comparison with others – may also be useful to ascertain changes in skills and learning over time.

References

Aitken, S. and Millar, S. (2000) *Listening to Children with Communication Support Needs.* Edinburgh: Sense Scotland and CALL Centre.

Birnbaum, R. and Deutsch, R. (1996) 'The use of dynamic assessment and its relationship to the code of practice: Working across boundaries'. *Educational & Child Psychology* 13 (3), pp. 14–24.

Blosser, R. and DePompei, R. (2003) *Pediatric Traumatic Brain Injury: Proactive Intervention*, 2nd edn. New York, Delmar: Thompson Learning.

Deutsch, R. and Reynolds, Y. (2000) 'The use of dynamic assessment by educational psychologists in the UK'. *Educational Psychology in Practice* 16 (3), pp. 311–331.

Haywood, C. H. and Lidz, C. S. (2007) *Dynamic Assessment in Practice: Clinical and Educational Applications.* New York: Cambridge University Press.

Hooper, S. (2013) *Assessment Practices and Procedures in Children and Adolescents with Traumatic Brain Injury.* Youngsville: Lash & Associates Publishing.

Limond, J. and Adlam, A. R. (2015) 'Cognitive interventions for children with brain injury', in Reed, J., Byard, K. and Fine, H. (eds) *Neuropsychological Rehabilitation of Childhood Brain Injury.* Basingstoke: Palgrave Macmillan, pp. 82–105.

Middleton, J. (2000) 'Applications in child mental health'. *The Psychologist* 13 (1), pp. 27–29.

Sternberg, R. and Grigorenko, E. (2002) *Dynamic Testing: The Nature and Measurement of Learning Potential.* Cambridge, UK: Cambridge University Press.

Ylvisaker, M. (ed) (1998) *Traumatic Brain Injury Rehabilitation: Children and Adolescents,* 2nd edn. Boston, MA: Butterworth-Heinemann.

Ylvisaker, M. and Gioia, G. (1998) 'Cognitive assessment', in Ylvisaker, M. (ed) *Traumatic Brain Injury Rehabilitation: Children and Adolescents,* 2nd edn. Boston, MA: Butterworth-Heinemann, pp. 159–179.

Ylvisaker, M., Hartwick, P., Ross, B. and Nussbaum, N. (1994) 'Cognitive assessment', in Savage, R. and Wolcott, G. (eds) *Educational Dimensions of Acquired Brain Injury.* Austin, TX: Pro-Ed, pp. 69–120.

Understanding and supporting behaviour changes

The loss of behavioral control is a reaction to an impaired brain attempting unsuccessfully to understand a complex environment. It is an attempt to simplify or alter the environment to the level that the head injured child or adolescent is able to manage appropriately and minimize behavioral expressions of confusion, frustration, or failure. Rarely can these procedures be identified or implemented by the head injured child or adolescent directly. Instead these techniques depend on other people to evaluate what specifically is overwhelming the head injured child, monitoring the environment for the head injured child, and implementing procedures to reduce the environmental complexity.

(Lehr 1990)

Changes in personality and behaviour are common following ABI. Of all the difficulties that may occur, families rate behaviour change as the most persistent, disruptive and disturbing of problems (Ylvisaker et al. 2005). Poorly controlled behaviour has a detrimental impact on adjustment to family, education, community activities and social life. Without support and help, unacceptable behaviours may persist, get worse over time and continue into adult life, increasing the risk of mental health disorders, anti-social – including criminal – activities, and difficulties maintaining relationships and vocational pursuits.

Behavioural challenges are often, over and above any other presenting problem, also the most difficult to tolerate in education settings and the most significant barrier to integration and to learning. How a student behaves, rather than how much he learns, can frequently be what determines the suitability or success of a placement. Changes in behaviour following ABI do not often resolve quickly or spontaneously. Also, generally, the longer the student experiences them, the harder they are to remediate and the more severe they can become.

Teachers often fail to associate behaviour difficulties with an ABI, especially if there has been any time lapse between the injury and the presenting behaviours. As described in Chapter 3, there may be delayed deficits resulting from injury, and behaviour difficulties may not emerge until months or even years after the trauma.

An understanding of a young person's brain injury and the impact that this can have on cognitive, communicative and psychosocial functioning enables those within education to be aware of potential difficulties and therefore make provision to avoid or to minimise them.

Behaviour at acute stage of recovery

Stages of cognitive improvements and related behaviours immediately after an ABI that has resulted in coma have been well documented, and descriptions of these stages, or levels of disability, have been organised into scales, e.g. the Rancho Scale (Malkmus and Stenderup 1974) and the Disability Rating Scale (Rappaport et al. 1982). References to these may be helpful during early stages of recovery to help explain the long-term processes of improvement from serious brain injuries. In the acute stages after injury, young people are often confused and agitated, as described in Chapter 2. Beyond the acute stages of recovery, more persistent, longer-term behaviour changes may emerge due to deficits in complex cognitive and psychosocial areas of functioning. It is these enduring, and sometimes later-emerging problems, that create barriers to academic and social success.

Longer-term behaviour difficulties

Behaviour changes can range from subtle difficulties to those that are considered to be very disruptive and challenging. Many of the expressions of these changes displayed by young people with ABI are also exhibited by those who are non-injured, but the frequency and intensity may be much greater in the young person with ABI and the antecedents may vary.

Common behavioural difficulties following ABI can include:

Impulsivity	Immaturity
Disinhibition	Inflexibility
Poor motivation	Irritability
Anger outbursts	Aggression
Dependency	Sexual inappropriateness
Stubbornness	Egocentricity
Denial	Emotional lability
Apathy	Lethargy

Some of the above issues relate to excesses of behaviour, but it is also important to appreciate that there can be a reduction of behavioural responses as a result of brain injury, which can also be challenging to educators. Damage to brain mechanisms responsible for arousal and initiation can be manifested as apathy or lethargy, and students may be described as lazy or lacking in motivation. There is often an assumption that the ability to attend and to initiate tasks is automatic and therefore any failure to do so is a wilful decision on the part of a young person. Also, apathy or lethargy are not generally deemed to be as problematic for educators as the managing of disruptive behaviours, because there is not such a negative impact on other individuals, nor does it necessarily divert a teacher's attention to the extent of being unable to deliver a planned lesson. There may, therefore, be less attempt to address the needs of students who are passive.

It is important to appreciate that significant limitations in behavioural responses can be just as problematic because they can interfere with successful learning and socialising as much as any excesses of behavioural response.

After ABI, there may be few if any behaviour changes or there may be many. Some young people may grow out of certain behaviours and go on to develop more appropriate ways of responding, or else the behaviours may be replaced by equally inappropriate but different ones. The intensity and frequency will also vary depending on a number of factors. There can be different reasons why they occur and an understanding of these can help to manage them effectively. Invariably, most behaviours are a complex mix of factors and the result of interaction between the student and the school or college, the family, and the wider community. However, ABI often creates additional issues that contribute to behaviour changes and difficulties.

Reasons for behaviour change after brain injury

Neurological damage to the brain

Injury to the brain and abnormalities in brain functioning can result in direct behavioural consequences. The parts of the brain responsible for self-regulatory mechanisms are commonly injured, resulting in reduction of ability to control behaviour. Disinhibition, impulsivity, reduced anger control, aggressiveness and other socially unacceptable behaviours can be observed in young people with ABI. These consequences may be delayed and may emerge when the executive skills appropriate to the typical developmental age and stage fail to mature.

Pre-injury behaviour problems

It is important not to assume that unwanted behaviours following acquired brain injury are a reflection of pre-injury characteristics. A large proportion of children and young people experience new and persisting behaviour problems after injury, associated with other factors, but there may be a continuation and/or magnification of behaviour problems experienced before the injury. There is much research to indicate that personality styles, behaviour patterns and family dynamics influence behavioural outcomes following ABI (e.g. Anderson et al. 2014). Although it is commonly believed that young people with behaviour difficulties are at increased risk of traumatic brain injury due to their inability to predict consequences, and therefore may be more accident prone, research indicates pre-injury behaviour does not significantly increase the risk of sustaining a brain injury (McKinlay et al. 2010).

Psychological reactions associated with disability

Many behaviour changes observed after an ABI are not a direct consequence of the injury but of the circumstances following it, particularly the young person's reaction to this and to the changes that have occurred as a result of it. Of most significance is the ability to deal with significant loss and change, e.g. loss of friends and social status; loss of independence; loss of previous academic and cognitive abilities or levels of success; and loss of physical function. These can all have a profound impact on a young person's emotional state and self-image. The student may no longer have the ability to function the way he did before and therefore not have control over situations that he previously had. Feelings of failure and frustration can lead to acting out or withdrawal. Students may demonstrate strong emotional outbursts as a reaction to what they consider to be unreasonable restrictions on desired activities. Cognitive deficits after ABI, such as impaired judgement, impulsivity or disinhibited behaviour, can lead to a young person's greater risk-taking. Prevalence of traumatic brain injury in the youth justice system is high – as much as 60% – and brain injury has been found to increase the risk of offending (Williams 2012). This raises concerns, particularly among parents, about safety issues, but close supervision by adults may be resented. This often becomes an increasingly contentious issue between parents and their child with ABI as the normal expectation for independence increases in adolescence. Safety issues around contact sports, road sense, drugs and sexual behaviour are common sources of friction, and any perceived intervention, control or restrictions by a parent can lead to an escalation of a child's or adolescent's behavioural outbursts.

Environmental factors

The family environment plays an important part in the development of all children and young people, including developmental changes of children and young people following ABI. As previously mentioned, there are many studies to indicate that the influence of the home can be a contributory factor towards behavioural outcome after brain injury (Wade et al. 2016). There is a much greater risk of increased, or new behavioural difficulties – i.e. problems that did not exist prior to injury – in young people with home environments that include significant psychosocial adversity (Ylvisaker and Feeney 1998). Young people with brain injury are more dependent on a positive and supportive family environment (Taylor et al. 2002).

Parents may have limited resources to respond to new problems, or they may already be too burdened by other stressful issues to be able to provide opportunities that encourage positive behavioural adjustment. Relevant support and information for parents are important parts of the rehabilitation process. Education staff too can provide a supportive environment with help to develop resilience in young people through opportunities to increase their feelings of self-esteem and experiences of success.

Cognitive and communicative impairment

Behaviour problems can be associated with difficulties young people have in understanding what is required of them; a lack of ability to carry out requested tasks; or feeling too tired to process and respond effectively. Situations can demand more skills than a student has the capacity to cope with – e.g. they may be too demanding, confusing or over-stimulating. The range of cognitive deficits that they now experience can result in a high level of frustration, which increases the negative behaviours. Feeney and Ylvisaker (1997) indicate that cognitive, behaviour and communication problems following brain injury are frequently 'alternative descriptions of the same underlying reality' – i.e. what is termed inappropriate behaviour may be due to increasing academic demands; communication deficits; problems with planning and organising goal-directed behaviour; lack of insight about limitations; forgetfulness; inability to transfer behaviour that has been learnt from one context to another; or rigidly sticking to ways of doing tasks that were successful in the past. Assessment and understanding of the young person's cognitive and communicative strengths and difficulties can help to inform ways of providing appropriate support.

Medication

Anti-convulsant or other medication may affect a student's learning capabilities and behaviour. There may also be a number of interrelated factors if changes are noted when young people are taking medication, all of which will need to be appraised. Any such concerns should be discussed with the family doctor as well as with other education staff.

Communicative intent of behaviour

'There is typically an important purpose served by behaviour, no matter how unusual or objectionable that behaviour may appear' (Feeney and Ylvisaker 1997). Almost all conscious behaviours are a way of communicating. A young person's behaviour is a way of coping with the world and its frustrations. Students with ABI may have verbal communication deficits along with a range of cognitive difficulties, and these are exacerbated by fatigue, anxiety, confusion, disorientation, etc. Whenever any of these negative feelings are experienced, it is often not possible for him to talk fluently enough to express this, or to say what he would like to have changed. Behaviour is often his only language; he does not necessarily choose to misbehave but may not possess any other skills under certain conditions.

When a student is experiencing behaviour difficulties, it is important to consider what message he may be trying to convey. For instance, it may be to express: boredom; that the work is too difficult; a need for attention; a delight in getting a reaction which is entertaining; a feeling of being tired or overwhelmed; a measure of control; or frustration because of unpleasant comments from peers. Identifying the communicative intent is a first step towards providing alternative, more positive ways to replace unwanted behaviour.

Supporting behaviour in an educational environment

Teaching and helping students in the classroom to behave in socially acceptable ways is an integral part of the wider educational process for enabling young people to be as independent as possible.

By law, all state schools in England are required to make arrangements for the safety and welfare of their students. This includes publishing a behaviour and anti-bullying policy, which parents are entitled to have a copy of on request. A clearly written and understood behaviour policy that is applied fairly and consistently can encourage a calm, orderly environment and respect for one another.

Although some of the behavioural difficulties seen in young people with ABI may need to be addressed differently from those of others, clear expectations for appropriate behaviour should always be maintained. This, therefore, is not at odds with approaches to behaviour management which are planned and agreed at a whole school or college level. Parents, students and staff all need to be aware of the clear procedures for supporting behaviour.

There is increasing recognition of the benefits of whole school or college positive behaviour supports. This is characterised by concern for the well-being of the students, staff, parents and the wider community with the aim of changing the environment and culture. Creating a positive learning environment where children and young people are welcomed; feel safe, valued, respected and included; and can develop a sense of connectedness or belonging can provide an important and long-term protective role in nurturing good mental health and appropriate behaviour.

Use of consequences

Approaches to behavioural support in schools and colleges may involve consequential strategies.

Having consequences in place is essential for the successful running of an organisation. Most people learn to behave according to expected consequences, i.e. they do what is likely to result in something that is rewarding, or they avoid doing something that could have an unwanted outcome for them. Behaviour management policies and practices in schools and colleges commonly include principles that focus on delayed consequences (Department for Education 2016). These are typically sanctions that are applied if rules are violated. There also needs to be emphasis on positive consequences, i.e. outcomes for students who comply with rules.

Consequential management of behaviour is linked to an assumption that young people have intact neurological mechanisms for:

- an understanding of cause and effect
- remembering what they have to do to achieve or to avoid a particular outcome
- understanding that a particular outcome may be delayed, i.e. exercising some degree of self-control
- being able to generalise from one situation to another.

Students with ABI may have lost these cognitive skills, which are rarely clearly identified because, for most people, they are part of an automatic or effortless repertoire that has been gradually acquired or learnt during developmental progress.

The use of **positive consequences** is very important; all students need to be acknowledged and rewarded for appropriate behaviour, including those with ABI. However, the behaviour of students with ABI needs to be managed and supported primarily by antecedent control (see page 90).

Students, parents and all education staff need to know what the consequences are for misbehaviour, and this must be part of a whole-establishment policy. It is important to understand, though, that **negative consequences** do not help students with ABI to behave appropriately. Some strategies commonly used in classrooms may even exacerbate the very behaviours that they aim to eliminate. Reprimands given when a student is already experiencing a high level of stress or excitement can result in an explosive outburst.

Delayed consequences are commonly ineffective for managing behaviour provoked by ABI: they may fail to act either as a 'brake' for inappropriate behaviour or as an incentive to behave in desirable ways because:

- Difficulties with memory, organisation of thoughts and with problem solving may mean that potential consequences cannot be anticipated, i.e. they are often not able to choose a course of action based on what is likely to happen later.
- ABI frequently damages the parts of the brain responsible for monitoring and inhibiting behaviour, so providing few internal resources for control. When a

student with ABI begins to lose control, there is an inverse capacity to self-regulate this, i.e. the more he loses control, the less able he is to stop what he is doing. When behaviours begin to escalate, more resources are required of the adult in charge. 'It is like the proverbial water going over the dam. Once behaviours begin to escalate it is more difficult for teachers and parents to manage the behaviours' (Savage et al. 2001).

- Delayed reprimands often have little meaning for students with ABI, who may have limited recollection about the events for which they are being admonished.

- The use of sanctions, by themselves, does not help students learn more appropriate behaviours.

> Murray had been hit by a car when he was 9 years old and sustained an ABI. He made a good physical recovery and was very keen to get back to school to rejoin his friends. At age 13, he was attending a mainstream comprehensive school. He was described as below average ability, disorganised and forgetful. He was generally liked by staff, but viewed as immature and silly by peers. He was often teased and called names because of his slowness to respond, especially when a topic of conversation had moved on and his verbal contributions to discussions were considered to be inappropriate or irrelevant. Murray was sensitive to criticism and reacted aggressively, mostly verbally but sometimes physically, which tended to happen when no adult was in earshot to keep name-calling at bay. On one occasion in class, Murray had been 'wound up' excessively, resulting in him physically lashing out at another boy. The two of them were sent to see the deputy head teacher, who was busy and so they had to wait until he was free to talk to them. By the time this happened, Murray had very limited recall of the classroom dynamics that had led to the assault, but was asked to describe in detail what had happened, which he was unable to do. The other teenage boy was able to provide an articulate account of himself as a 'victim' of an unprovoked attack, which then engendered further agitation and verbal abuse from Murray. This lent additional credibility to the 'victim's' account and to Murray being perceived as the troublemaker. He was denied privileges and put on report.

Prevention

Preventing problems before they occur, or interrupting behaviours before they escalate, is about managing environments to enable students to control their behaviour and to experience success. **Antecedent control** is a positive, proactive approach, as opposed to reacting to problems, i.e. dealing with them after they have happened. If internal mechanisms for regulating behaviour have been damaged or destroyed, then there is a need for external supports to help students to behave appropriately. Focusing on the antecedents that are most likely to cause an escalation of unwanted behaviours, and managing the environment to prevent them from happening, is much more effective than expecting the young person with ABI to remember the rules and to abide by them. Antecedent management of behaviour:

- reduces or eliminates unwanted behaviours
- creates a more calm, positive and productive working environment for everyone
- gives a young person greater control of the environment
- allows a student greater accomplishment and success
- provides many other long-term benefits – e.g. raised self-esteem
- removes the focus on punitive action
- teaches adaptive skills to all students.

Understanding the brain injury and the impact it has had on a student's cognitive functioning helps education staff to use strategies that prevent, or minimise, problematic behaviour from either starting or escalating out of control. The most effective way to do this is to predict when unwanted behaviours are likely to occur. Knowing the triggers enables environmental changes to be made that will minimise the likelihood of that behaviour occurring.

Consistent approach

Behaviour rarely changes overnight, and some students may have had years to develop ways of behaving that are inappropriate. Young people's behavioural repertoires can also be very limited if they have lost the skills that had served them well prior to injury. There are also no such things as 'quick-fix' behavioural programmes or solutions. Education staff may claim they have 'tried everything' but that nothing has worked. They may have tried strategies with which they are familiar as being effective for other students with uninjured brains. It may also be the case that several different strategies have been used, but each of them only for a short time, or only when the member of staff has remembered to use them, or only by some of the adults who work with the student. Consistency is crucial to help those with ABI learn to behave appropriately, and this can only happen if everyone applies the same rules in the same way. It also encourages greater understanding and support among colleagues. Shared concerns and support are crucial for individual members of staff to feel confident in handling difficult situations in the classroom. If a strategy appears to be unsuccessful, it is important to examine the extent to which consistency is being applied:

- Do all members of staff have the same expectations for behaviour in any given situation, such as in the classroom, the dining hall, the playground or leisure areas, in the corridors, on the school bus, etc.?

- Are expectations clearly defined for students and staff, leaving no ambiguity about interpretations of what is appropriate, i.e. what actually must be seen to constitute appropriate behaviour? A student with ABI will benefit from being reminded of the rules and expectations each time a particular situation is about to occur.

- Are there frequent verbal and visual opportunities for everyone to be reminded about the rules of behaviour? Are they prominent in visual form, such as in an eye-catching notice on every classroom wall or other situations specific to the relevant behaviour? Students with ABI may genuinely not know how to behave in certain situations and will often take their cue from other information around them. If the only cue is another student behaving inappropriately, they may well follow suit.

- Are rewards applied consistently? It is far more preferable to focus on appropriate behaviour and reward it than to give more attention to undesirable behaviour. It enhances the positive atmosphere in the class and is usually very reinforcing. Even students who frequently display unwanted behaviours are appropriate some of the time, which makes it all the more important to acknowledge the times they are doing so.

- Are all students rewarded? Students with ABI need encouragement, recognition and reinforcement about acceptable ways of behaving.

- Do students and staff know what the consequences are for breaking rules? These must not be subjectively decided by individual members of staff, but must be part of an agreed whole-establishment policy, i.e. a planned rather than an impulsive approach.

- Are sanctions applied consistently? Students can quickly get to know the members of staff who threaten sanctions for misdemeanours but who never carry them out or do so inconsistently. This increases the likelihood of continued inappropriate behaviour.

- Is rule breaking consistently handled calmly?

Functional assessment of behaviour

> No matter how bad a child's behaviour seems, it is important to remember that most children are driven to succeed and that at any given time they are probably doing the best they can with the abilities they have.
>
> (Deaton 1994)

Behavioural assessment and behaviour change are not processes that are 'done to' or 'carried out on' a young person, nor are they to be confused with crisis management. A behavioural assessment involves understanding what triggers particular behaviour in a context; ascertaining what the communicative intent or function of the behaviour is; and identifying the environmental, instructional, affective and other factors that appear to lead to and maintain the behaviour (see Chapter 6). This information enables changes to be made to enhance the probability of increasing appropriate behaviour and decreasing problematic behaviour. Most behavioural assessments and interventions in the classroom are low-key, quick to implement and immediately rectify situations that are considered inappropriate, e.g. the class teacher may see a student becoming quickly overexcited and not attending to task when papers start blowing around the classroom due to a draft. The situation can be easily rectified and the student redirected after closing the window or door. More systematic, structured functional assessment is required when behaviours frequently interfere with the learning or safety of any of the students in class.

Changing aspects of a young person's behaviour need to be carefully considered within a collaborative problem-solving process; in other words, it is important to involve all relevant members of staff, parents and the student, if it is age-appropriate to do so. This establishes a team approach to acknowledge the situations in which there are unwanted behaviours. Mutual respect and co-operation is vital in managing behavioural problems as well as acceptance that all concerned have an important role to play. Directly involving the student and family as much as possible can increase their motivation for changing situations and for understanding the reasons for doing so. Knowing how a young person behaves at home and the strategies that are successful there may provide useful insights when trying to ascertain appropriate interventions in the classroom. Also, parental endorsement of a behavioural programme and reinforcement at home can increase consistency and therefore the likelihood of success. To change behaviour, it is crucial to carry out an assessment of the behaviour and the factors that contribute to it. A common mistake is to try to implement a strategy before going through the processes set out below.

Specify the behaviour

To change behaviour, it is necessary to specify exactly what the student does that needs to change. Words such as 'lazy', 'disruptive', 'rude', 'aggressive' and 'hyperactive' may sometimes be considered useful shorthand in general conversation, but the terms do not indicate what the behaviour is. Descriptions such as 'gets out of seat many times during the lesson', 'shouts obscenities when asked to do a writing task' and 'swings his arm out and strikes another student that he passes in the corridor' are behaviours that can be observed and measured. Care needs to be taken when choosing words to describe behaviour to make sure that everyone in the team understands and also that they do not apportion blame. There may be a number of unwanted behaviours, but it is important to prioritise and attempt to change just one or two behaviours at a time. Also, focusing on the implementation of a positive behaviour can sometimes reduce a number of other undesirable behaviours if they directly compete with it. For instance, Janine frequently does not carry out the tasks she is asked to do, gets out of her seat many times during the lesson, wanders around the classroom, talks to other students, starts to fiddle with equipment and other materials in the room, and shouts out comments about other students' work that is on display. There are a number of different behaviours there! Identifying one of the behaviours to change, such as getting out of her seat during lesson time, will inevitably have a knock-on effect on the other disruptive behaviours; if she stays in her seat, she is not carrying out the other disruptive actions.

Identify the features of the behaviour and those associated with it

Behaviour almost always serves a purpose and takes place in an identifiable context. The contextual setting, what happens before a particular behaviour, and what immediately follows the behaviour are important in order to ascertain what is maintaining this. A-B-C approaches to recording behaviour are so called because they:

A – describe **ANTECEDENTS** to the behaviour, i.e. events which occur prior to it and which may trigger it
B – describe the specific **BEHAVIOUR**
C – describe the **CONSEQUENCES** of the behaviour, i.e. the events which immediately follow it and which may reinforce it.

Other direct observations in the settings in which the unwanted behaviour occurs are important to record as well, as they may help to explain the reasons for this.

Keeping records of what is observed is necessary for successful behaviour change. Accurate information is required prior to implementing a behaviour-change strategy in order to establish:

- how long the behaviour continues each time it occurs – its duration
- how many times it occurs – its frequency
- where and when it occurs
- who else is there
- what is going on at the time the behaviour occurs.

Once a system has been agreed and established for daily observations of behaviour, recording does not have to be time consuming or complicated. It may be helpful to draw up a simple chart. Collaboration and consultation between staff are likely to increase willingness of staff to use such a chart.

Identify the purpose of the behaviour

It is important to consider the communicative intent of the student and the ways in which the behaviour benefits him, e.g. gaining attention, avoiding a task, or sensory stimulation. Often the function of a behaviour is:

- to avoid or escape from something – e.g. a task, a person or an event
- to obtain something – e.g. attention, control or a particular activity
- to express a feeling – e.g. discomfort, excitement, anxiety or surprise.

The purpose of a behaviour is not always immediately evident, and so gathering more information about the student and the wider context can help to ascertain what function it serves.

Identify the contributing factors: the wider context

In addition to the specific and immediate contextual events – i.e. the antecedents to the behaviour – assessment information for behaviour change needs to include a wider appreciation of the environmental, instructional and personal factors, such as those listed in Chapter 6, as examination of these may help to explain the reasons for the behaviour. Some of these may not necessarily be factors that can be changed, e.g. fatigue, but an understanding of them can help to determine the most appropriate ways to support a student with ABI.

To understand the wider context, it may be necessary to gather information from many different sources using a variety of methods, e.g. observation, the student's education records, behaviour checklists, interviews with the student, the parents and other members of staff.

Summarise information and make hypotheses

After the information has been gathered, it should be discussed with parents and relevant staff and a hypothesis drawn up about the student and the behaviour. A hypothesis is a suggested statement about the relationship between the behaviour and other factors.

> e.g. When this occurs . . . Jennifer does . . . in order to . . .

The information and hypothesis can help to focus further questions that may enable those involved to understand and address unwanted behaviour.

> e.g. Does the student have the skills to meet the demands of the situation in which the problematic behaviour occurs?
>
> Do the other students sitting close by help or hinder the situation?
>
> Does the behaviour only happen at certain times of day and in certain places? Are there additional health or family factors?

A student's angry outbursts may be triggered by a request to carry out a piece of work, but an appreciation of the overwhelming fatigue that is experienced by some people with ABI may indicate that to be a significant factor.

A summary of the information can be agreed upon to include:

- why the behaviour occurs – e.g. Jennifer finds it hard to concentrate
- the conditions relating to the behaviour, the triggers and the context, i.e. what prompts it – e.g. when Jennifer is asked to do written work in the afternoon. Additional factors are other students around Jennifer who snigger and make faces to one another because of the difficulties she has in class; they enjoy the entertainment value in watching her become increasingly agitated
- the consequences – e.g. Jennifer gets angry or upset, sometimes cries, and avoids doing the written tasks
- other factors in the classroom and at home – e.g. Jennifer becomes easily frustrated with her homework and gets angry, shouting abuse at her siblings in the evenings when she has homework

Develop and implement an intervention plan

The team needs to decide how the learning environment can be changed to address the issues, with the focus on proactive strategies. The plan should identify alternative behaviour and this may need to serve the same purpose as the one to be eliminated, e.g. to enable the student to exercise some control or to gain attention, but in a positive and acceptable manner. It must also state the positive strategies and supports that need to be put into place. Strategies need to:

- be collectively agreed
- be easy to implement
- be the least intrusive possible
- have a positive impact on the student and all others in the environment

    e.g.   Jennifer has a rest after lunch in a designated quiet area. She changes the place where she sits in most of her classes.

    She is provided with short achievable tasks and given frequent encouragement. When her class has written work to complete in the afternoons, Jennifer is given a differentiated worksheet in a multiple-choice format. This eliminates the necessity to generate ideas, which she was having problems with when tired, and to produce written text.

    She is provided with a drink and small snack during mid-afternoon break.

    She transfers five minutes early between classes, and at the end of the afternoon before the corridors get busy.

Members of staff and her parents were delighted with the considerable improvements that these changes made to her behaviour, and also to her work.

Determine effectiveness of intervention

After implementing agreed strategies, previously gathered information allows judgements to be made about whether a behaviour is changing over time, i.e. whether it is decreasing or increasing. Many behaviours do not change rapidly, and systematic recording may be the only way to discern small but gradual changes. These can amount to bigger changes over time, and a record can be useful to encourage continued implementation of particular strategies and to ensure that these are not abandoned prematurely. It is important to seek the opinions of the whole team regarding the effectiveness of the intervention plan and whether it should be continued or a different strategy considered.

Responding to behavioural incidents

It is important to intervene in the setting when and where the behaviours occur. Talking to the student in some other location following a time delay may not be helpful; the young person with ABI may have forgotten about a specific incident and also may have difficulties in making a connection between what is being said in one setting and his behaviour in another. However, sometimes it is not possible or appropriate to address a behavioural incident at the time it occurs, in which case it will be necessary to calmly remind the student about the incident, out of the hearing of others, and provide explicit instructions about how he should behave.

Do not ask a student with an ABI to explain the reasons for his inappropriate behaviour, but redirect him. A child or adolescent with ABI, whose behaviour is beyond acceptable limits or is escalating towards this, is not feeling calm or relaxed! Students with ABI show limited self-awareness and have difficulty analysing and monitoring their own behaviour. Their ability to problem-solve or to organise their thoughts is even more limited when they are tired or anxious. This will also make it hard for them to recall the events that triggered their inappropriate behaviour, no matter how short the time span. This is not the time to reprimand. Do not argue or discuss at this point; redirect the student to another activity within the room or, if emotions have been running high, allow him to go to a quiet place where the level of stimulation is low. This can provide time for him to calm down, free from the stress factors in the classroom. If a reprimand is necessary and the student is already agitated, do this when he is calmer; use a tone of voice that is firm, quiet and devoid of emotion. Make statements rather than ask questions, placing the emphasis on the appropriate behaviour to be displayed under these circumstances, i.e. state exactly what he must do next time. Avoid nonspecific comments such as 'behave yourself' or 'try being good for a change', which give no clues to how a student should behave.

Respond in a calm, neutral manner. Maintain eye contact, and use verbal and body language – tone, volume, words, stance, etc. – that are emotive-free. Do not over-react. It is very important that the adults in charge are in control of their own feelings, as any expression of anger or irritability will only serve to increase the student's anxiety and negative reactions.

The least restrictive strategy for managing behaviours must always be used.

Do not simply react to what is observed. Remember that behaviour is a manifestation of other difficulties. It is important to ascertain the reasons for a student's inappropriate response.

Time Out

'Time Out', in behavioural terms, is an extreme form of ignoring inappropriate behaviour where the young person is removed for a brief period of time from the group or class to an area which is devoid of stimulation to give opportunity to calm down. It is a non-rewarding strategy and based on the principle that the student will want to return to the usual setting which is more interesting and desirable, and hence will behave in a way that enables a return. Time Out usually means time out from opportunities to be positively rewarded. It is sometimes used as part of a programme for managing very challenging behaviour of young people in special settings, some of whom have behaviour difficulties following acquired brain injury, and it has associated implications for resources, safety and the young person's well-being and, therefore, needs to be managed very carefully.

The expression 'Time Out' can sometimes be used in a loose way to describe different ways of managing behaviour, and so it is important to establish a shared understanding of the term in any context and ensure responses are consistent. 'Time Out' should not be confused with the need for young people with ABI to have a quiet place in school where they can go to relax or to calm down, away from the stimulating classroom environment (see 'Quiet place of rest' below).

Quiet place of rest

A student who is struggling to make sense of a situation may have difficulties filtering out the range of stimuli common in busy classrooms and trying to understand and to remember what is expected of him, and these difficulties can quickly create a build-up of negative emotions. A range of factors can lead to behavioural outbursts that represent a way of the student saying, 'this is all too much for me, I can't cope'. Punitive action is not desirable or effective, but the student may well benefit from moving away from a situation which has become overwhelming. It is important that a student with ABI has access to a safe place in which to rest or work, which has a low level of stimulation, when the classroom conditions are more demanding than he can manage.

Additional behavioural issues following ABI

Post-Traumatic Stress Disorder (PTSD)

PTSD in young people following traumatic brain injury has yet to be extensively studied. There can be a wide range of emotional and physical reactions displayed following any severe traumatic event and PTSD can be experienced by both adults and children. Symptoms such as flashbacks, nightmares or frightening thoughts – especially when exposed to events or objects reminiscent of the trauma – and sleep disturbance, depression, anxiety, irritability or anger outbursts may be experienced. PTSD in young people with traumatic brain injury is complicated, because many symptoms overlap with those resulting from the brain injury. Central to a diagnosis of PTSD is the re-experiencing or recollection of the event in memory. There has been some belief that PTSD and TBI are incompatible because most survivors of TBI have no conscious recollection of the events surrounding their trauma. However, there has been some indication that PTSD can occur after TBI in children and adolescents (Max et al. 1998) and that 'pseudomemories' can have the same impact on emotions as actual ones (Bryant and Harvey 1998).

Pre-existing family problems and the family's reaction to a young person's injury may affect the course of PTSD (Crouchman 1998). As previously indicated, there can be a number of factors following ABI that influence strong emotional reactions, such as frustration, anger, sadness, anxiety and depression. They may or may not be related to re-experiencing the traumatic event that resulted in the injury. However, it is important not to dismiss these, whatever the source, and any negative emotional reactions need to be addressed as part of the rehabilitation process. An Australian web-based brain injury organisation, Synapse – see the Useful organisations and resources section – provides further information about symptoms of PTSD, its association with ABI, possible treatment options, and further reading on the topic.

Denial and lack of self-awareness

Very often young people with ABI do not recognise that they have any difficulties as a result of their brain injury, although these can be very obvious to others. They may be unable to appreciate that their behaviour causes offence to others, and they may have unrealistic expectations and anticipate a resumption of their pre-injury lifestyle, despite a range of significant physical or cognitive deficits. Young children can also experience a lack of awareness because of developmental limitations.

Denial and lack of self-awareness are not the same, although frequently the distinction is not made and the terms are used interchangeably. Lack of awareness can be due to a neurological deficit that is a direct result of damage to specific parts of the brain, resulting in an inability to understand. Strictly speaking, denial indicates an awareness of that which is being denied. Denial can be a psychological coping mechanism that serves a very important function of enabling an individual to manage what could otherwise be an overwhelming amount of distressing change. Although this may be healthy during a period of readjustment, long-term denial can be problematic. It can place young people at greater risk of further injury or abuse, because they do not accept their own vulnerabilities and therefore are unaware of the need for increased safety vigilance. There can be resistance to or a lack of motivation for any additional help or compensatory strategies within education because they do not see the need for any intervention.

Confronting individuals, either parents or their children, who experience denial or limited self-awareness is rarely helpful and can lead to even more severe reactions to the injury. Increased awareness of one's own deficits has sometimes been associated with reactions such as substance abuse or depression. Recommendations for working with the issues of denial (Savage and Pearson 1997) are based around opportunities for young people to experience their difficulties as well as their strengths in a supportive environment, with adult help to encourage strategies and consideration about what is needed to experience success, rather than trying to prove that there are problems. Skilful questioning on the part of education staff can enable a young person to focus on strengths and the progress that has been made, and gradually to think about areas that are difficult.

Adolescent behaviour

Sometimes it can be unclear, particularly to parents and educators, as to what constitutes inappropriate adolescent behaviour. Frequent mood swings, angry outbursts, a lack of co-operation and communication, impulsive behaviour and testing the limits of adult authority are features that can be related to an ABI, but also are not uncommon features in adolescence.

> He was going through adolescence before all this and we found it hard going, especially his younger sister who got just as much of his bad behaviour as we did but wasn't old enough to understand the changes in adolescence. Now it is much, much worse. There are arguments every day. He flies off the handle at the slightest thing. We can't get him to co-operate and do any household jobs. We have to make sure he and his sister virtually live separate lives. He doesn't consider anyone else at home except himself and makes demands which, if they're not immediately met, cause him to get into a rage. Life at home as well as at school is so different now and I can't say that any of us are happy. We sometimes ask ourselves if that is how it would have been anyway, even if he hadn't had his accident, or is it because of that?
>
> (Parent of a child with ABI)

If there is a known brain injury, it is important to consider the following, adapted from Savage and Pearson (1997):

- Is the behaviour now different in range, intensity and frequency than before the injury?
- Is it different in range, intensity and frequency than that of others of a similar age?

- Does the adolescent seem frustrated?
- Do the problems seem related to memory, attention, initiation and organisation, as well as impulsivity and poor judgement?
- Has the adolescent maintained the same peer group as before the injury?

Reference to current books on adolescence and adolescent behaviour can provide additional information as to what is considered typical development.

Sexual behaviour following ABI

Brain injury can have a direct impact on sexuality, or it may have none at all. An adolescent may experience sexual development that is considered within the typical range; their sexual interests, drive, experiences and socialisation may not be unduly different from those experienced by their peers. Sexuality is thought about and manifested in many different ways, such as in the way individuals create their appearance – their clothes, hair, cosmetics, etc. – how they regard their feminine or masculine persona and how they behave towards others. Adolescence is normally a time associated with increased interest in sex and sexuality and it is not unusual for sexual feelings to be strong in both boys and girls, regardless of a brain injury. Rapid physical and emotional changes and a wish to develop greater autonomy and independence from the family can increase the desire to engage in exciting and risk-taking behaviour. ABI often increases those risks. Physical, cognitive and social changes can disrupt normal sexual maturation and behaviour in a number of different ways:

- Precocious puberty – i.e. earlier than experienced within the broad 'normal' range. This must be a medical diagnosis (see Chapter 4).
- Physical deficits can affect a young person's self-image or the way he is viewed by others, or place limitations on his ability to engage in sexual activities.
- Social isolation from peers that frequently occurs after ABI can result in a young person being cut off from what is, for many adolescents, the main source of information about sexual matters.
- Impaired judgement and disinhibition can result in highly inappropriate behaviours, including:
  - unwanted, excessive or obsessive sexual comments and innuendoes – unwanted touching of another person
  - indiscreet masturbation
  - sexual exploitation either by, or of, others.

Sex and relationship education is compulsory in England from the age of 11 years, and all schools must compile a policy in relation to this which is available to parents. However, a young person's disinhibited behaviour, and increased vulnerability to abuse or exploitation, are unlikely to be adequately addressed in usual curricular activities. Appropriate sexual behaviour relies on many skills that the adolescent may no longer possess. The power of a sexual drive in someone who has memory difficulties, poor awareness and limited mechanisms for self-control may mean that particular issues or situations require direct and structured intervention in order to minimise risks. Education staff and parents need to share any concerns they have and if necessary draw up a behaviour plan. Additional strategies may need to be taught and reinforced on every occasion in which there is heightened risk. See the Useful organisations section for sources of information that provide more in-depth detail about a range of sexuality issues.

Depression

Education staff must be aware that students with ABI, particularly adolescents, are at increased risk from mental health difficulties following ABI (Green et al. 2013). Social skills are highly valued in adolescence and a young person may be aware of his differences and his difficulties in maintaining the kind of social relationships that he used to enjoy, and he can become overwhelmed and depressed. Teachers must be alert to changes in behaviour that may indicate depression, such as even greater levels of disorganisation, inattentiveness and isolation; decreased stress threshold; chronic fatigue; crying; or mention of suicidal thoughts. Any concerns should be immediately discussed with a relevant clinician so that the young person can be evaluated for depression and receive treatment if this is needed.

References

Anderson, V., Spencer-Smith, M., Coleman, L., Anderson, P., Greenham, M., Jacobs, R., Lee, K. and Leventer, R. (2014) 'Predicting neurocognitive and behavioural outcome after early brain insult'. *Developmental Medicine & Child Neurology* 56 (4), pp. 329–336.

Bryant, R. and Harvey, A. (1998) 'Traumatic memories and pseudomemories in post traumatic stress disorder'. *Applied Cognitive Psychology* 12, pp. 81–88.

Crouchman, M. (1998) 'Recovery, rehabilitation and the neuropsychological sequelae of head injury', in Ward Platt, M. and Little, R. (eds) *Injury in the Young*. Cambridge: Cambridge University Press, pp. 263–299.

Deaton, A. (1994) 'Changing the behaviors of students with acquired brain injuries', in Savage, R. C. and Wolcott, G. F. (eds) *Educational Dimensions of Acquired Brain Injury*. Austin, TX: Pro-Ed, pp. 257–275.

Department for Education (2016) Behaviour and Discipline in Schools. Advice for Headteachers and School Staff (www.gov.uk/government/publications Reference: DFE-00023–2014).

Feeney, J. and Ylvisaker, M. (1997) 'A positive, communication-based approach to challenging behavior after ABI', in Glang, A., Singer, G. and Todis, B. (eds) *Students with Acquired Brain Injury: The School's Response*. Baltimore, MD: Paul H. Brookes, pp. 229–254.

Green, L., Godfrey, C., Soo, C., Anderson, V. and Catroppa, C. (2013) 'A preliminary investigation into psychosocial outcome and quality of life in adolescents following childhood traumatic brain injury'. *Brain Injury* 27 (7–8), pp. 872–877.

Lehr, E. (1990) *Psychological Management of Traumatic Brain Injuries in Children and Adolescents*. Gaithersburg, MD: Aspen Publishers.

Malkmus, P. and Stenderup, K. (1974) *Levels of Cognitive Functioning*. Downey, CA: Rancho Los Amigos Hospital, Communications Disorders Service.

Max, J. E., Castillo, C. S., Robin, D. A., Lindgren, S. D., Smith, W. L., Sato, Y. and Arndt, S. (1998) 'Posttraumatic stress symptomology after childhood traumatic brain injury'. *Journal of Nervous and Mental Disease* 186 (10), pp. 589–596.

McKinlay, A., Kyonka, E. G., Grace, R. C., Horwood, L. J., Fergusson, D. M. and MacFarlane, M. R. (2010) 'An investigation of the pre-injury risk factors associated with children who experience traumatic brain injury'. *Injury Prevention* 16 (1), pp. 31–35.

Rappaport, M., Hall, K. M., Hopkins, K., Belleza, T. and Cope, D. N. (1982) 'Disability rating scale for severe head trauma: Coma to community'. *Archives of Physical Medicine and Rehabilitation* 63 (3), pp. 118–123.

Savage, R. C. and Pearson, S. (1997) 'Common questions when serving students with ABI', in Glang, A., Singer, G. and Todis, B. (eds) *Students with Acquired Brain Injury: The School's Response*. Baltimore, MD: Paul H. Brookes, pp. 369–383.

Savage, R. C., Pearson, S., McDonald, H., Potoczny-Gray, A. and Marchese, N. (2001) 'After hospital: Working with schools and families to support the long term needs of children with brain injuries'. *Neurorehabilitation* 16 (1), pp. 49–58.

Taylor, H. G., Yeates, K. O., Wade, S. L., Drotar, D., Stancin, T. and Minich, N. (2002) 'A prospective study of short-and long-term outcomes after traumatic brain injury in children: Behavior and achievement'. *Neuropsychology* 16 (1), pp. 15–27.

Wade, S., Zhang, W., Yeates, K., Stancin, T. and Taylor, H. G. (2016) 'Social environmental moderators of long-term functional outcomes of early childhood brain injury'. *Journal of the American Medical Association Pediatrics* 170 (4), pp. 343–349.

Williams, W. H. (2012) *Repairing Shattered Lives: Brain Injury and Its Implications for Criminal Justice*. London: Barrow Cadbury Trust.

Ylvisaker, M. and Feeney, T. (1998) *Collaborative Brain Injury Intervention*. San Diego, CA: Singular Publishing Group Inc.

Ylvisaker, M., Turkstra, L. and Coelho, C. (2005) 'Behavioral and social interventions for individuals with traumatic brain injury: A summary of the research with clinical implications'. *Seminars in Speech & Language* 26 (4), pp. 256–267.

Social supports

Existing literature confirms that parents of children with TBI [traumatic brain injury] often report poor social adjustment (i.e. smaller friendship networks, increased behaviour problems, poorer social skills).

(Moran et al. 2015)

Prior to injury, a child or adolescent may have formed some clear concepts of his own identity and personal expectations, acquired through his life experiences and interaction with others, e.g. 'I'm good at sport because I'm on the school football team'; 'I have some very good friends; we get together at break time and we meet up at weekends'. A sudden loss of skills and abilities can quickly lead to dramatic changes in a person's experiences, which are no longer able to provide confirmation of the self-concepts he may have previously developed. A rapid decline in friendships, social activities or social standing, or perceived 'status' in school or college, e.g. in terms of academic or sports prowess, can lead to emotional and psychosocial problems, such as lowered self-esteem, social isolation, lack of confidence and sometimes depression, particularly as many young people can remember how they were before their injury. ABI can have a dramatic impact on peer relationships. Loss of friendships is reported by many parents whose children have experienced changes following their ABI – at the very time they desperately need peer contact and support.

Most children learn to understand social cues at an early age. They are commonly learnt intuitively or incidentally, rather than as a result of formal instruction. Studies have indicated that skills of social competence, or the impairment of them, are developmentally linked and are probably directly associated with executive function maturation. A study by Karver et al. (2012) showed that a younger age at injury indicates the increased risk of difficulties with social skills later during childhood. ABI in older children or adolescents can also result in sudden loss of, or problems in using, the knowledge and complex skills involved in social interaction that have been developed over the young person's lifetime.

Friends who initially offered support after the injury all too frequently drift away. Initiating and maintaining new friendships is problematic. As with many of the behaviour changes after ABI, the social and emotional difficulties are often related to cognitive deficits. In particular, changes to cognitive-communication skills and executive functioning make it hard to process complex social situations. This can affect social interactions and relationships.

Young people with ABI often have little insight into the reasons why their peers no longer choose to interact with them. Also, friends, peers and others commonly lack the skills required to successfully continue a positive relationship with someone who may appear unusual or unpredictable. They often find it difficult to understand how someone with no visible evidence of problems can now be so different.

Difficulties which contribute to social rejection may include:

- inability to engage effectively in a balanced two-way or group conversation because of disorganised thinking, slow speed of processing information, reduced comprehension and difficulties initiating conversation
- loss of ability to understand jokes, metaphors or sarcasm, as well as non-verbal communication
- impulsive, disinhibited behaviour, including 'silly', immature responses
- invading personal space – standing too close to others or touching them
- insensitivity to the needs and feelings of others, such as making offensive remarks
- problems with processing abstract and subtle language.

Social rejection exacerbates a young person's difficulties because it precludes opportunities for him to practise social skills that might lead to greater social inclusion.

Many young people with ABI become more dependent on their families for social support and contacts. Studies of young people who have acquired brain injury indicate that significant loneliness is not uncommon (Prigatano and Gupta 2006). Young people who are lonely are at risk of poor adjustment in adult life and may be at increased risk of getting involved in criminal and delinquent behaviours.

In order to relearn social skills that a young person may have had prior to injury, as well as to develop new skills, it is necessary to assess the deficits first. This cannot be done effectively by psychometric testing or behavioural/social skill rating scales alone. A neuropsychological assessment may indicate deficits in cognitive skills desirable for social success, but the additional environmental factors inherent in social interactions make it essential to include contextual observations, reports and discussions with those who know the young person well. It is also important to determine whether the nature of any difficulties stems from a lack of skill acquisition, or problems in using skills which may already have been acquired. There is a distinct difference between the two, and the strategies used to teach desired social skills which are not already part of a student's behavioural repertoire are different from the strategies needed when he already possesses the skills but fails to use them. For instance, coaching, modelling or direct teaching may be useful approaches for teaching a new skill; reinforcement and motivational strategies may be more relevant if skills have already been learnt.

Five key classroom intervention approaches for helping students who are lonely have been identified by Pavri (2001), and these may be useful for students with ABI:

- social skills training
- creating opportunities for social interaction
- creating a positive educational climate
- teaching adaptive coping strategies
- enhancing student's self-esteem.

The activities mentioned below have been loosely grouped under these approach headings. They have not been devised by the authors, nor have they been especially designed to use with children or young people with ABI. They have been gathered from a range of sources and have been successfully used with young people with ABI. Any of these kinds of approaches could be included within a PSHE – personal, social, health and economic education – curriculum and within the SRE – sex and relationship education – aspect of this for which there is documented government guidance in the UK.

Social skills training

Since the early 1990s, there has been a proliferation of social skills training packages, some of which are excellent, and there has been much success in teaching social skills to students. The much more difficult task for those with ABI is to learn when and where it is appropriate for them to use the skills. Learning social skills needs to involve a step-by-step approach, augmented by demonstration, role-play, practice and repetition. A student with ABI may have significant difficulties generalising what has been learnt and using this in 'real-life' situations, so it is very important that the skills are rehearsed and practised repeatedly in his natural environments, i.e. the actual settings in which the skills need to be used. The following strategies may usefully be considered:

- Discuss the rules of interaction regularly. In order for change to occur, a one-off teaching or training period is not enough. Explicit teaching of skills and competencies with much opportunity to demonstrate the skills needs to be ongoing.
- Use positive reinforcement selectively directed to encourage a desired behaviour, building on strengths and competencies. Most people respond to compliments and students with ABI should be praised for simple, expected social behaviour that is usually taken for granted in others.

- Teach specific scripts of common behaviours for situations in which they are frequently expected – e.g. saying good morning; saying please or thank you; giving eye contact to the person who is speaking or is spoken to.

- Encourage imitation of positive behaviour. Young people may learn much about ways to behave by observing and copying someone else's behaviour. This can be a powerful device when the young person identifies with the individual he is aspiring to model, but negative models can be just as highly influential as positive ones. Consideration must be given to the appropriateness of the behaviour demonstrated by the model. The effectiveness will also depend on how motivated the student is to imitate the behaviours and how much opportunity he has to observe and to practise the desired behaviours. A young person will not be influenced by observation if he is unable to remember what he has observed. For this to be used to effect, input is required from an adult who is able to help him to clearly identify the relevant features that could be copied and for them to be put into practice, rehearsed and repeated in his normal settings.

- Consider self-modelling. This is a technique described by Kehle et al. (1997) and has been found to be even more effective. This involves the careful filming and editing of the young person on video, exhibiting only appropriate behaviours, including both verbal and non-verbal aspects of communication. This can occur either through role-playing and prompting for the purposes of the video, or by recording real situations but editing out inappropriate or negative behaviours. The student is then able to watch his own appropriate behaviour in situations which are problematic for him, with an adult who is instrumental in the behaviour change verbally reinforcing what is seen on video. The pause and replay functions of videos can be helpful for analysing behaviour. Attention is only drawn to elements in communications that are successful and that can be built on to help make wanted changes. Repeated exposure to the information on video and frequent opportunities to practise the behaviours in everyday settings can enhance the learning opportunities.

A relatively recent video feedback approach that is gaining interest and use in the UK is Video Interactive Guidance (VIG; Kennedy et al. 2011). VIG-accredited trainers work in a variety of settings, including in schools and with parents. The process starts with negotiation and collaboration about desired social communication changes. Personalised interventions are used by building on each individual's learning style and skills. The focus is always on strengths and potential, not problems or difficulties.

However, extreme caution is required when considering video feedback approaches as some young people who have experienced significant change, especially visible changes, as a result of an acquired injury, and who remember how they were previously, may find video images of their new selves distressing.

Sara suffered a severe traumatic brain injury at the age of 15 when she was in a road traffic accident while travelling by bus on a school outing. After her acute care in a large regional hospital, she was transferred to a residential rehabilitation facility. She made excellent physical and cognitive recovery of many skills. While staying there, she enjoyed much attention from her wide extended family, staff and celebrities who coincidently were visiting the rehabilitation facility at the time she was there. She also received much attention from representatives of the local media in her home area, who had taken her cause to heart and were campaigning for safety measures to be put into place on the section of road where the accident occurred. Her school staff had maintained close contact throughout her absence, making regular visits to see her and sending cards and recordings to remind her of school activities. Her return and early reintegration to school was well supported and successful, both academically and socially. She had become quite a celebrity herself! Her friends had been helped to adjust to the changes in Sara, which was considered to contribute to the maintenance of positive peer relationships. About six months after her return, overall progress continued to be very encouraging, but there were reports about the reduction in the quality and quantity of peer interactions. When given opportunity to express their feelings, her peers indicated their considerable irritation about Sara's ongoing expectation to be the centre of attention. They felt that they had made many allowances and adaptations for her after her return and were willing to go on doing so, but they were fed up with the daily behaviours that Sara displayed every time she entered a room whereby she expected to be the centre of attention and to be made a fuss of, but never showed an interest in others around her. This issue was very sensitively addressed by her tutor as part of a wider social skills programme in which Sara was involved. Like many of the other subtle social skill difficulties that she now displayed, she was oblivious to the impact of her behaviours on her peers and lacked sensitivity to the needs of others. More desirable behaviour was practised in role-play and then, with the agreement of Sara and her parent, she was videoed in one of her classrooms so that she could watch herself interacting in a more socially balanced way. She watched this with her tutor on a few occasions and the recording was also used to help demonstrate and reinforce a number of additional features relating to social communication that Sara had lost. These were part of the normal repertoire of her peers, but were among the factors that 'make her different', as one of them said.

- PATHS (Promoting Alternative Thinking Strategies) is one example of a social skills training package that can have application for students with ABI as well as for a whole primary school approach. It is a process developed in the US by Greenberg and Kusche and reported by Hindley and Reed (1999). It is aimed at promoting the development of the social and emotional skills that underpin social problem-solving and was initially devised for use with deaf students, but has been introduced into mainstream primary schools in the UK, for the benefit of all students. It places an emphasis on visual learning materials which, for a student with ABI, can help to augment verbal learning strategies. PATHS covers five areas of social and emotional development: self-control, self-esteem, understanding and recognition of emotions, peer relations and social problem-solving skills.

Creating opportunities for social interaction

Generally, young people can be very supportive when they are given accurate information to help them to understand the changes in their classmate and are allowed to help problem-solve. Without information, peers can be confused and lack the skills to communicate with someone who does not fit into their perceived 'norm'. They, too, need to be provided with new, additional skills or else they will withdraw their communication efforts. However, group strategies are ones that enable all students to benefit. They promote positive peer relationships as well as connect young people with caring adults. Members of staff have a critical role to play in providing a supportive environment where students do not feel that they may be rebuffed or ridiculed if they get it wrong. The following strategies may be useful:

Buddy systems

Buddies are peer helpers with whom the young person can be paired up to help provide an informal support network. A 'buddy' needs to be a good role model who is supportive, tolerant and empathic and who has volunteered to 'look out' for the student during more unstructured times – e.g. break and lunchtimes; on the school bus; transitions between classes – or who sometimes helps to carry books and other materials. There needs to be more than one assigned buddy, and a 'Circle of Friends' (see the next section) may be a preferable option. Alternatively, buddies may be assigned for particular tasks, e.g. a 'study buddy'. It is essential that none of the volunteers feel a burden of responsibility. They also need to know that they can discuss any concerns they have about their role with an identified member of staff on a regular basis. Buddies may need particular guidance in knowing how to respond to unusual or unexpected behaviours that can occur with their peers who have an ABI.

Circle of Friends

A Circle of Friends is something that is often taken for granted by those who have one. Students with ABI all too often lack this kind of supportive network. For a young person who does not have a natural circle of friends, a social support network can be created by members of staff who facilitate the circle process. 'Circle of Friends' is a strategy devised by Pearpoint et al. (1996), in which a network of peers choose to develop and maintain a friendship group that supports the notion of acceptance and mutual benefit and includes the student who lacks social contacts. Members of the friendship circle may look out for the young person with ABI at break times, transfer classes with him, attend leisure or sporting activities with him, etc. The process is one that can develop from a whole-class activity on the topic of friendship, discussing the nature of friendship and the perceptions and feelings of others who have few or no friends.

Friendship Stop

This has been established in the playground of some schools for younger children and is a place where any child can go to sit. Children are 'primed' to keep an eye on the stop and to include any child there in their own activity or just to go and chat with them. Some schools have children who volunteer to be on a rota in order to monitor the Friendship Stop. Schools 'set the scene' with explanations to ensure that no one feels different or stigmatised by using it, helping children to understand that many of them will experience some playtimes or situations that are difficult and a Friendship Stop is a facility for everyone in the school who wishes to use it. Continued reinforcement of those explanations is very important to ensure that lonely or socially excluded children are not unintentionally further disadvantaged.

Community participation

The student should be actively encouraged to be involved with youth groups in the local community, the nature of which will depend on interests and access skills. A young person with ABI may try to cling onto the belief that he continues to be included in the same social group of which he was a part prior to his injury, but this may no longer be the case. He may benefit from help to understand that friendships come and go, and that making new connections can provide him with new possibilities.

Consultation

Consulting with parents can help teachers develop a deeper understanding of the social and emotional difficulties a student may be experiencing. Collaboration is also useful to identify leisure or sporting activities that may be appropriate for the young person. Wilson and Newton (2006) describe a group problem-solving process using the circle model – a Circle of Adults. A Circle of Adults who closely work or care for the young person, such as parents and teachers, can contribute to a better understanding of a young person's emotional and behavioural needs when a more in-depth exploration may be beneficial, and collaborative support strategies are generated. A range of problem-solving circle-based interventions are provided by Grahamslaw and Henson (2015).

Creating a positive educational climate

Ensuring the social and emotional well-being of students is a fundamental pre-requisite for successful learning for all children and young people. Schools and colleges have been increasingly identified as providing not only formal academic learning opportunities, but also for developing social and emotional well-being and resilience. A whole school or college approach is characterised by concern for the well-being of the students, staff, parents and the wider community. Education staff play an important part in nurturing a sense of belonging, where all students are welcomed and feel safe, valued, respected and included, and where there is acceptance of difference and diversity.

A useful strategy towards promotion of this in schools is Circle Time. This is based on the principle of everyone in a school community learning to listen to one another, to take responsibility and to work towards a positive school ethos. Jenny Mosley (1999), the author of a number of books on Circle Time, emphasises that it is 'no good creating oases of respect in the classroom . . . if the other policies do not also foster and ensure respect for both children and adults'. She has devised a 'Whole School Quality Circle Time Model', which is aimed at meeting the needs of all individuals in the school. A Whole School Quality Circle Time approach includes the provision for the times of the school day when specific difficulties are most likely to occur, e.g. lunch and playtimes can be problematic because of their unstructured nature. Circle Time can involve the teaching of playground games, the provision of playground zones supervised by older students, and activities for those who need more structure.

Nurture groups

Nurture groups were originally set up in mainstream primary schools to provide a short-term nurturing environment for children who find it difficult to learn and respond appropriately in their classroom (Boxall 2002). The success of such groups has encouraged secondary schools to adopt and adapt the concept. Part of a whole school approach to supporting young people with social and emotional difficulties, nurture groups provide a predictable structure and routine within a 'homely', comfortable, relaxed setting, and are designed to enable a small group of young people to learn, socialise, prepare and share meals together. There are clear expectations about behaviour such as waiting, taking turns, sharing, etc., which can lead to increased learning, independence, social skills, self-esteem and ability to remain in mainstream education (Sanders 2007).

Teaching adaptive coping strategies

The predominant issue of loss, already referred to, is one that is extremely hard for a young person to adjust to without help. It is not surprising that students with ABI are often affected by emotional disturbance because of all the changes to their life and lifestyle. Opportunities for regular counselling can provide a way of assisting a young person to manage the difficulties he perceives as well as being a safe setting in which to express his feelings. He may benefit from having an opportunity to discuss fears, worries, relationships, sexuality and other intimate issues, free from fear of disclosure to peers, parents or members of staff. A range of counselling approaches may need to be considered, and Lehr (1997) emphasises the importance of tailoring the interventions to the student's skills and changing needs. The focus may be, for example, on managing conflict, understanding the changes that have occurred, planning for transitions, making new friends, etc. Individual counselling may be what is required at a particular time, but group, family or sibling counselling may also be useful to consider.

Unfortunately, most people who offer counselling services do not have any training or experience in working with children and adolescents with ABI. It is essential that anyone who offers this kind of support acquaints themselves with the core issues of ABI and the deficits and limitations of the individual young person in order to maximise opportunities to communicate effectively. The adult in a counselling role must have appreciation of why a young person with ABI may respond differently from one with a brain that is neurologically intact. Considerable sensitivity and adaptation is often required, taking into account the possible changes to a young person's communications, in particular significantly reduced verbal skills. Traditional approaches for 'talking therapies' may not be appropriate or useful.

It is important that young people with ABI have an identified member of staff with whom they can link up at least once a day. Ideally this should be someone with whom the young person feels he has a positive relationship. This person can assess how well the youngster is coping by meeting with him daily and gathering observations from other members of staff.

Enhancing young people's self-esteem

MAPs (Making Action Plans), which is devised and described by Pearpoint et al. (1996), is a collaborative planning process that involves the 'key actors' in a young person's life. The student, his family, any particular peers, teachers and other significant people meet and discuss the student's and the family's personal dreams and goals, and together they think of ways of making them a reality by drawing up an action plan and following it through. The key issue that is addressed is: what does the young person and family want? This is a powerful process because it involves the people who are already key figures in the young person's life, collaborating and negotiating specific steps to create and effect a plan of action.

References

Boxall, M. (2002) *Nurture Groups in Schools: Principles and Practice*. London: Sage.

Grahamslaw, L. and Henson, L. H. (2015) 'Solving problems through circles'. *Educational Psychology in Practice* 31 (2), pp. 111–126.

Hindley, P. and Reed, H. (1999) 'Promoting Alternative Thinking Strategies (PATHS): Mental health promotion with deaf children in school', in Decker, S., Kirby, S., Greenwood, A. and Moore, D. (eds) *Taking Children Seriously*. London: Cassell, pp. 113–132.

Karver, C. L., Wade, S. L., Cassedy, A., Taylor, H. G., Stancin, T., Yeates, K. O. and Walz, N. C. (2012) 'Age at injury and long-term behavior problems after traumatic injury in young children'. *Rehabilitation Psychology* 57 (3), pp. 256–265.

Kehle, T. J., Clark, E. and Jensen, W. R. (1997) 'Interventions for students with traumatic brain injury: Managing behavioral disturbances', in Bigler, E., Clark, E. and Farmer, J. (eds) *Childhood Traumatic Brain Injury*. Austin, TX: Pro-Ed, pp. 135–152.

Kennedy, H., Landor, M. and Todd, L. (2011) *Video Interaction Guidance: A Relationship-Based Intervention to Promote Attunement, Empathy and Wellbeing*. London: Jessica Kingsley.

Lehr, E. (1997) 'Counseling students with ABI', in Glang, A., Singer, G. and Todis, B. (eds) *Students with Acquired Brain Injury: The School's Response*. Baltimore, MD: Paul H. Brookes, pp. 277–292.

Moran, L., Bigler, E., Dennis, M., Gerhardt, C., Rubin, K. H., Stancin, T., Taylor, H. G., Vanatta, K. and Yeates, K. (2015) 'Social problem solving and social adjustment in pediatric traumatic brain injury'. *Brain Injury* 29 (13–14), pp. 1682–1690.

Mosley, J. (1999) *More Quality Circle Time*. Cambridge: LDA.

Pavri, S. (2001) 'Loneliness in children with disabilities: How can teachers help?'. *Teaching Exceptional Children* 33 (6), pp. 52–58.

Pearpoint, J., Forest, M. and O'Brien, J. (1996) 'MAPs, circles of friends, and PATH', in Stainback, S. and Stainback, W. (eds) *Inclusion: A Guide for Educators*. Baltimore, MD: Paul H. Brookes, pp. 67–86.

Prigatano, G. P. and Gupta, S. M. C. (2006) 'Friends after traumatic brain injury in children'. *Journal of Head Trauma Rehabilitation* 21 (6), pp. 505–513.

Sanders, T. (2007) 'Helping children thrive at school: The effectiveness of nurture groups'. *Educational Psychology in Practice* 23 (1), pp. 45–61.

Wilson, D. and Newton, C. (2006) *Circle of Adults*. Nottingham: Inclusive Solutions (www.inclusive-solutions.com).

CHAPTER 9

Planning educational provision

The educational experience can be more appropriate if educators take individual differences into account, analyze the learning tasks that must be accomplished, determine those student behaviors that contribute to success or non-success, create a learning environment conducive to the student's needs and selectively apply a variety of teaching techniques and strategies.

(Blosser and DePompei 1994)

As previously explained, the educational needs of students with acquired brain injuries are frequently complex, sometimes not easy to identify and generally different in nature or in combination from those of other students with additional needs. This, therefore, presents a challenge for those planning to meet these needs.

Sometimes the needs of these students may appear to be similar to those of others and, therefore, interventions that have been successful for other students may be appropriate. However, the difficulties faced by those with ABI can easily be open to misinterpretation and often require unique and explicit programmes of intervention.

It is important for parents and students to be reassured that teachers have the skills necessary to devise and oversee appropriate programmes for students with ABI. Most have specific experience of working with students who have Special Educational Needs (SEN) for other reasons and can use this knowledge. However, in order to do this appropriately, they will also need:

- information regarding ABI, with guidance regarding the most common manifestations of potential difficulties
- specific information about the individual student in question. Detailed information regarding assessment and identification of these needs is included in Chapter 6, but immediate information can also be sought from the student or his parents and from medical and therapy staff or clinical psychologists who may have been involved with him.

Good practice dictates that information regarding a student's additional or different needs and the ways in which these will be addressed should be clearly documented.

Previously in England there was a requirement in state-maintained schools for students with identified special educational needs requiring different types of intervention to be provided with an Individual Education Plan (IEP), devised and monitored within the school – IEPs are very different documents in other countries, such as the USA. Due to legislative changes in England, educational establishments are no longer required to produce IEPs – although there is a recommendation by the Department for Education that some form of school-based plan is formulated; but there is now a recognition of needs potentially through to 25 years of age.

Many English schools do continue to produce IEPs for their students, but alternative documents may be termed Additional Needs Plans, Provision Maps, Support Plans, Profile and Outcome Plans, or Personal Learning Plans, etc.

There is different use of terminology in Scotland, Wales and Northern Ireland, with new legislation in Wales removing the term Special Educational Needs (SEN) to be replaced with Additional Learning Needs (ALN). All learners with ALN will have an Individual Development Plan (IDP). A new framework planned for Northern Ireland may also alter currently used terminology.

Although there are differences throughout the UK, as in other countries, there is a trend towards longer-term and more comprehensive provision being made for children and young people with special educational needs and disabilities, to involve health, social care and educational services.

Whatever the particular system is that exists where the child or young person with ABI is receiving education, there are basic principles that can be followed and issues that must be considered when planning appropriate provision to meet needs and to enable optimal progress and achievement.

Planning

Comparison with other students

Sometimes it may seem that these young people do not have significant additional needs. Education staff may comment that there are other students in the class who appear to have much greater levels of difficulty and for whom additional intervention may seem to be more clearly indicated. Quite understandably, as there are enough demands on staff towards meeting diverse needs within an inclusive curriculum, they do not want to create additional concerns or burdens when these are unnecessary. However, as the student with ABI is likely to have some preserved areas of ability in addition to acquired problems, and a store of previously acquired knowledge and skills, he may well have considerably more potential than he can demonstrate without additional support and resources. His overall achievements may not be significantly worse than some of his peers, but it is only relevant to compare these young people with their own previous and current potential, not with other students.

John was 6 years old when he suffered a traumatic brain injury in a road traffic accident. Three years later, he was achieving at a very low level in school, but no particular concerns were raised and he was not in receipt of any significant additional support or resources. The head teacher insisted that he had no particular difficulties and had no acquired problems as a result of the accident. He said John's levels of ability and concentration were in line with that of his siblings and also said he had taught John's father years previously who had been similar. The class teacher said John had never concentrated well, rarely completed tasks without prompts, and that they joked in class that he was a 'daydreamer', and she and the other children often called to him to come back to Planet Earth! John laughed with them about this.

Investigation revealed that John has post-traumatic epilepsy and was suffering from absence seizures. He also has other significant acquired attentional problems in addition to difficulties with organisation and initiation. When these were recognised and addressed, his achievements increased significantly.

John's academic performance was no worse than some of his peers who also had attention difficulties in class, nor did he present as a child with behavioural difficulties; but with the knowledge of his acquired brain injury, his performance was considered in a different light. This enabled his difficulties to be recognised and therefore addressed.

Prediction of needs

It is important to realise that ABI frequently leads to learning difficulties, although not necessarily apparent ones when the student first returns to school. Many, like John, do not appear to have significant needs during their earlier school years, but their difficulties – and the differences between them and their peers – become much more pronounced as they progress through the education system. This can provoke much more significant learning and, sometimes, behavioural difficulties, as a result of prolonged failure and frustration or changes in demands during teenage years and beyond. These can be avoided if difficulties are acknowledged and addressed as early as possible. Comparisons can be made here with students with developmental dyslexia with whom most members of education staff are now familiar. Sousa (2001) also refers to students in schools with 'dual exceptionality',

> whose abilities and disabilities mask each other. They . . . are considered average students, and do not seem to have any problems or any special needs. Although they may seem to be performing well, they are in fact functioning well below their potential. In later high school years, as course work becomes more difficult, learning difficulties may become apparent, but their true potential will not be realised.

Too often, when a student returns to school following an acquired brain injury and seems to be making such a good recovery, a 'wait and see' policy is adopted. However, with an awareness of the potential effects of such an injury, it is not reasonable to expect him to reintegrate without considering how this injury may affect his access to the curriculum and his potential.

> At 10 years of age, David was said to have made a 'remarkable' recovery from a serious TBI. He returned to his mainstream school placement with no specific additional support/differentiation. He was initially referred for a statutory assessment of his special educational needs, but this was then withdrawn when further assessment found he had regained age-appropriate levels of achievement. He soon transferred to the next stage of his education and began to show increasing difficulties with work and, more particularly, with behaviour. His behaviour was addressed in an unsuccessful and punitive way, and David was permanently excluded. He transferred to a special school but his individual acquired needs as a result of his brain injury were not considered. Eventually he faced the possibility of permanent exclusion again, but additional non-teaching assistance was provided in order for him to remain in school. However, his individual needs were still not addressed and there continued to be significant difficulties. David withdrew from the school before his fifteenth birthday.

David has the intellectual ability for achievement in public examinations, and if there had been an early understanding of his *different* difficulties and the challenges that he would face as he continued through school, he may have had greater opportunity to realise his potential. As it was, his behavioural and psychological difficulties compounded and increased.

'Invisible' deficits

Damage caused in acquired brain injury is not visible. If the young person had suffered permanent damage to an area of the body, such as his dominant hand, it is likely that the problem would be immediately addressed rather than assumptions made that he would 'cope'. Comments regarding the fact that there were other students in the class who were also clumsy would not be made. No one would wait to see if not being able to write appropriately affected his educational potential or caused him problems before planning intervention. When targets were set for him, this would not be with the expectation that he could 'fix' his hand. 'To learn how to use his right hand to write legibly and at an appropriate speed' would not be set as a realistic target. If there was the possibility that he could regain some use of this with appropriate training or exercises, this may be incorporated into his programme, but in the meantime alternative means would be found to enable him to record his work. He would be provided with any necessary additional resources, along with training and support, in order for him to be able to use these efficiently. There should be no lesser consideration of injury to the brain and the loss or impairment of specific skills that it controls.

Compensatory strategies

As these students may have permanent deficits resulting from their injuries, some provision should focus on the development of compensatory strategies. An example of this could be a memory impairment. Some people have better memories than others and there is, therefore, a significant range of potential within the normal population. However, education staff often expect students to be able to make more effort, to work harder, or to find ways of remembering information, for instance for tests or exams. Assumptions may be made that some students do not spend enough time revising and, therefore, lack motivation or commitment. However, if his ability to remember is permanently impaired, regardless of how much time the young person spends trying to remember information in the way that his friends do and in the way that he used to, he will be unsuccessful. Being told to try harder is unhelpful at best and frustrating and provocative at worst. He needs to relearn different ways of maximising his ability and to have support to compensate for his deficits.

Gaps in educational progress

Even if a student has made subsequent improvement following an ABI, there may be gaps in the 'building blocks' necessary for future learning because of time in hospital and away from school, and cognitive difficulties. It is important to think about the 'gaps' in a student's education since his injury: gaps in experiential and direct learning; gaps in achievement; and gaps in social skills development and interpersonal relationships. It may be necessary to readdress skills or information that his peers have learnt in previous years.

Cognitive styles

Much has been written relating to 'brain-based' learning and cognitive styles. Individuals process and learn information in a variety of ways. For instance, Smith (2002) points out that 'Albert Einstein said numerical ideas came to him more or less as images that he could combine at will, whereas others have said they rely on verbal representations of numbers when thinking about problems'.

Issues relating to cognitive style are particularly important to consider in terms of the changes that may be faced by a student with ABI. It may be difficult for anyone to change preferred styles of learning, revising, remembering, etc., but acquired difficulties affecting specific skills may necessitate this, if previous approaches to learning are no longer efficient. It may therefore be helpful to identify key features of any new learning in which young people with ABI have been successful, and then to encourage and build on this.

Identification of needs

When considering the specific needs of those with ABI, information should be obtained from relevant teaching and non-teaching staff and, if appropriate, observation of the student. As referred to in Chapter 6, the questions when? where? and why? may be useful to ask in relation to difficulties that are identified. For instance, if a student has significant difficulties with concentration, or specific problems with reading, it is essential to consider if his performance is better or worse at different times, in different environments, or with different activities, etc.

It is helpful to consider what skills he needs in order to be able to complete a specific task, e.g.

- What skills does he need to be able to concentrate/to be able to read?
- Does he have some of these, but lack others?
- Do certain situations/environments/instructions enable him to achieve more?

Each curricular area and each activity within it will require a slightly different combination of underlying skills to enable the student to succeed. For instance, it is clear that different combinations of skills – controlled by different areas of the brain – are necessary in Maths depending on whether the task involves: 'mechanical' computations; numerical reasoning; geometry; estimation; data handling; algebra; rote learning of tables, etc.

An approach to the identification of difficulties must be analytical to enable appropriate target setting and intervention planning. When skills necessary to complete a task have been identified, problem areas often become apparent. It then can be clear why the student can complete one task but not another that superficially seem comparable, or can work in one environment but not another. The following checklist may serve to instigate this analytical process, although teachers may well add to or adapt this. Does the student demonstrate the following skills necessary for efficient learning at an age-appropriate level?

Ability to:

- attend to verbal and visual information
- ignore a reasonable level of distractions
- shift attentional focus
- multi-task to an age-appropriate level
- show persistence to complete a task
- generalise information or skills from one situation to another

- adapt to changes of routine
- process incoming information at an age-appropriate rate
- complete oral or written tasks at an age-appropriate rate
- retain information in working memory
- retain information in long-term memory
- retrieve information from memory
- problem solve to an age-appropriate level
- display appropriate motivation
- sequence tasks or activities
- display efficient visuo-perceptual ability to interpret information from within a complex page or background; recognise, match and differentiate visual symbols in literacy, numeracy, etc.
- display efficient visual ability – with or without aids
- indicate adequate hearing ability
- scan visual information efficiently
- display age-appropriate abstract reasoning
- demonstrate flexible thinking
- efficiently interpret social and non-verbal cues and behaviours
- be aware of own strengths and weaknesses
- retain an overview – not become lost in details
- initiate activities
- inhibit inappropriate actions or impulsive behaviours
- express information verbally
- express information in writing
- retrieve appropriate vocabulary for verbal and written communication
- display fine motor and pencil control skills – or alternatives with appropriate technology
- display efficient motor planning skills
- display appropriate gross motor skills.

Differentiation

In order to meet the needs of a student with ABI, it is important to remember that there may be a need for differentiation of any of the following:

- teaching methods
- curricular content
- materials
- environments
- expectations.

Information relating to specific strategies and provision is detailed in Chapter 10.

Documented plans to identify needs and detail intervention

Such plans must be useful, practical documents. They should be devised with the involvement of the student and his parents, if appropriate, along with members of teaching staff and the person responsible for special needs provision within the establishment.

They should include information regarding *what* should be taught, *how* it should be taught and *how often* it should be taught. For many students with ABI, the most important things that they need to learn in order to access the curriculum and to make academic progress are:

- strategies to overcome some of their acquired deficits – e.g. relating to memory
- new approaches to learning to take into account current strengths and weaknesses
- some specific skills that develop intuitively in others without brain injury, which may have to be explicitly taught to these students – e.g. some communication or planning skills.

Teaching of these skills may need to be on an individual basis. Depending on the nature and complexity of the young person's difficulties, this could be undertaken by either a teacher or a teaching assistant, under the direction of a teacher. It is very important that even though these skills may be taught and practised at specific times, they should be reinforced and prompted in all areas of the curriculum.

Formulating targets

The targets for these students may relate, for instance, to improving academic achievement in literacy or numeracy, but also to improvements in underlying skills or behaviour. The latter can be formulated as **SMART targets** – specific, measurable, achievable, relevant and time bound.

When targets are set for a student with ABI, it is important to consider terminology. Before formulating targets with the onus on the young person for improvement, thought must first be turned to the identified cause of the problem and consideration given to what is achievable. If the student has impaired attentional ability, he cannot improve this at will. However, with more of an onus on staff to provide means by which he can *maximise* his impaired attention, a target can be made appropriate. This should not absolve the student of responsibility to work towards his goals once he has been provided with the appropriate resources, strategies and opportunities to do this, but it does recognise his underlying disability. Targets should be clear, informative and unambiguous to *all* those who come into contact with him.

Identifying and understanding the underlying disability that causes the young person's difficulties is the best way of minimising some of the disabling effects of ABI. Addressing the root causes of the problem is generally successful in enabling the student to maximise his potential, e.g.

> **Why** is he slow to develop early reading skills?
> **Why** is Maths difficult?
> **Why** can he not understand concepts of turn taking?

The student with ABI may be seen to have difficulties or special needs in a relatively large number of areas. However, it is not appropriate to attempt to meet too many targets at one time, as this is too confusing and perhaps unachievable for both the young person and the staff. Identifying causes as well as manifestations can help to address a number of issues at the same time. However, if necessary, issues must be prioritised in order of importance.

Planning intervention

Many suitable strategies and methods will already be familiar to teachers of students with special educational needs. However, they may not be used to utilising them with young people presenting different profiles of strengths and difficulties. A small steps approach may be necessary or implementation of strategies used when working with students with other specific learning difficulties may be useful.

Some of these students may also benefit from specific peer support or involvement of a counsellor or mentor. This needs careful planning, however, and is referred to in Chapter 8.

Success criteria

Once underlying problems are identified, work towards ameliorating or compensating for those becomes the focus for the intervention, rather than curricular issues. The targets and methods, therefore, change, but the success criteria can still relate to the curriculum. For instance, if an underlying difficulty relating to attentional skills is identified, increasing this ability could be a target and ways of attempting to achieve this could be agreed, but the measure of success could be in terms of time spent on specific curricular tasks, such as numeracy or literacy.

Reviews

Once an initial plan detailing appropriate intervention has been agreed, it is important to review this after a shorter time than may normally be considered. This is partly because the student's needs are often complex and require different types or combinations of approaches which need more careful initial monitoring to evaluate their efficacy. The needs of students with ABI also often change more frequently than is the case for those with other learning difficulties. If targets have not been met, there must be consideration at the review of the appropriateness of both the target and the intervention. It may be that one or both of these requires revision.

Teaching assistants/learning support assistants

When planning any additional provision necessary for these students, consideration should be given to a range of other resources – including in-service training, non-contact time for teachers to plan and to prepare materials and IT resources – but *not* just to the provision of a laptop. There is also a valuable and useful role for teaching assistants.

As with all staff working in educational establishments, teaching assistants cannot be in a position to support students with ABI effectively without appropriate awareness raising and supervision.

The specific role and responsibilities of a teaching assistant in this respect should be clearly defined and justified.

The student with ABI may need:

- additional repetition and reinforcement of key information or skills to be mastered
- simplification of some verbally presented information
- presentation of certain information or instructions on an individual basis
- extra time to complete activities or pieces of work
- differentiation of written or visually presented information
- a quiet environment to work on certain tasks or to learn key facts
- provision of additional visual organising aids
- provision of verbal or visual cues or prompts
- practice at using strategies to compensate for impairments of, for instance, memory or organisational skills
- work within an individual programme towards improving specific skills for learning
- practice of, and assistance with, information technology (IT) skills
- physical help or supervision for certain practical tasks

- practice within a programme devised by an appropriate therapist
- someone to provide a key point of contact between home and school/college
- planned practice of social skills within a small group.

All of these areas of need could be supported by a teaching assistant working under supervision, with a clearly defined role and to a prepared programme of intervention. The keys to appropriate use of such an assistant are:

- efficient and clear initial assessment and planning
- appropriate consideration of timetabling and curricular breadth
- training and awareness raising for the assistant
- clearly defined role and goals
- adequate support and supervision
- provision of advance information from teachers
- adequate preparation time for the assistant.

Reference has been made previously to the fact that accurate identification of the student's needs is important. An assistant allocated to work with a young person with ABI will need these to be clearly defined and stated. The agreed strategies to address these must also be clear and unambiguous.

Timetabling and curriculum

If the assistant is to spend time working individually with the student to explain topics or to reinforce work previously covered, careful consideration of the timetable must take place. This intervention will need to be conducted at an appropriate time and place, i.e. a distraction-free setting and at a time of day when fatigue levels are not at their highest. It may be appropriate to consider reducing the number of curricular subjects in order to increase achievement and meaningful learning in other, selected ones.

Training

If an assistant is to work extensively or on a long-term basis with a student with ABI, this person should have access to appropriate information and training relating to the student's condition. This will be in addition to any other training and personal development work encouraged and planned for teaching assistants. As with teachers, there is frequently an absence of information in training towards qualifications for this job that relates to acquired brain injury.

Role definition

The expectations of assistants are often complex and demanding. It will be rare for this to include doing anything exclusively on behalf of the student; there are some instances when assistants are required to take notes or to write ones that the student dictates, but even this should not occur without prior thought and consideration of the reasons for this. Most often the assistant will be helping or enabling the student to access the curriculum by differentiation, repetition, rehearsal, etc., or by facilitating him to develop independent learning strategies.

Supervision

However skilled a teaching assistant is and however experienced, an assistant is not a teacher. All assistants should have regular support and supervision by appropriate teaching staff, who should review and monitor their work.

Advance information

A key role for assistants is often to produce differentiated visual or written material. This may just involve printing or copying worksheets, etc. in order to cut and paste the information onto separate sheets in more manageable amounts. It may involve enlarging diagrams or illustrations, removing them from the body of text, or using alternative labelling. It may involve adding additional headings, lists of key words or highlighting sections. In order to do this, the assistant will require copies of the material from the teacher in advance.

Sometimes, if a significant proportion of the information or instructions in a lesson is to be provided orally, an assistant may need to remove a student with poor attentional or language comprehension skills to a quiet area during this time and present the information in an alternative manner and environment. In order to plan this, the assistant will require notification of lesson content in advance.

Preparation time

Having received information from staff and being aware of other material that the student requires, e.g. organisational aids, the assistant must have sufficient non-contact time to prepare.

Working co-operatively

As previously mentioned, the role of the assistant within a classroom is a challenging one, as is the role of the teacher when working with and supervising an assistant. As more assistants are now employed within education, teachers are increasingly familiar with this role, but some still find this difficult and can be uncomfortable establishing an appropriate working relationship. It is important for the adults to have mutual respect and understanding of each other's roles and for the teacher to be confident to supervise and to direct the assistant when necessary. The teacher must respect the assistant's knowledge of the student and his difficulties and of the programme that has been agreed for him. It is appropriate for training to be provided for teachers regarding working with teaching assistants as well as for the assistants themselves.

References

Blosser, J. L. and DePompei, R. (1994) 'Creating an effective classroom environment', in Savage, R. C. and Wolcott, G. F. (eds) *Educational Dimensions of Acquired Brain Injury*. Austin, TX: Pro-Ed, pp. 413–451.

Smith, A. (2002) *The Brain's Behind It*. Stafford: Network Educational Press.

Sousa, D. A. (2001) *How the Special Needs Brain Learns*. Thousand Oaks, CA: Corwin Press.

CHAPTER 10

Classroom strategies

Rehabilitation and education professionals agree that good teaching strategies designed especially for students with ABI are necessary and essential.

(Blosser and DePompei 1994)

There are many well-established methods of working with students with special educational needs that are very appropriate to incorporate into programmes for those with acquired brain injuries. Some strategies for students with a range of difficulties, such as developmental dyslexia or dyspraxia, autistic spectrum disorders or ADHD may be relevant, but adaptations will obviously be necessary to suit each student's individual profile of needs. The purpose of strategies is to maximise the student's chances of experiencing success in the intended learning activity.

The following is not a comprehensive list, but provides ideas and suggestions, already 'tried and tested' in classrooms, that may be useful to consider for children and young people with ABI. Education staff may be able to think of many other suggestions to assist the particular young people with whom they are working. Decisions to use any of the following should only be made in the light of knowledge of an individual student's strengths and difficulties.

Physical and sensory

Gross motor difficulties

- Obtain advice from a physiotherapist
- Plan for inclusion in physical/sporting activities
- Allow sufficient time/space for activities
- Establish a protocol for negotiating crowded places
- Provide help for carrying objects and for practical lessons

Fine motor difficulties

- Obtain advice from an occupational therapist
- Consider alternative methods of recording work – not necessarily a laptop computer
- Provide support and/or adapted materials in practical subjects
- Provide grips for writing implements
- Provide clips or non-slip surfaces for stabilising writing paper
- Provide roller or gel pens for writing
- Ensure appropriate seating and table height

Ataxia or tremor

- Ensure good sitting posture when working: chair and table at correct height, sitting 'square' to the table, feet flat on the floor, elbows/forearms on the work surface, upper body leant slightly forward
- Allow student to sit rather than stand when appropriate

Visual difficulties

- Request information provided by any treating ophthalmologist or optician
- Obtain advice from specialist educational support services, if available
- Ensure optimal seating and lighting
- Use markers or guides to assist tracking when reading
- Provide high contrast for visual information
- Prompt the wearing of spectacles if prescribed
- Establish class rules for a 'clutter-free' room
- Determine optimal font size for text
- Allow extra time to complete tasks

Hearing difficulties

- Request information provided by any treating audiologist
- Obtain advice from specialist educational support services, if available
- Ensure optimal seating for listening
- Make eye contact when speaking to the student

- Minimise background noise
- Provide written information to accompany verbal instructions
- Ensure videos are subtitled or prepare notes in advance

Headaches

- Establish protocol in liaison with parents/carers or the student regarding use of analgesia, etc.
- Provide drinking water
- Monitor pattern, duration, severity, frequency of headaches and contact home if there are any changes
- If occurring at specific times – e.g. every Maths lesson – don't assume the cause to be an avoidance strategy; also consider other factors such as environmental ones, e.g. task difficulties, lighting, noise, etc.

Fatigue

- Ensure a graded return to education/time in the education setting after injury
- Timetable most-demanding tasks at optimum performance times if possible
- Provide breaks/rest periods
- Remember that offering a snack or meal can help
- Arrange for a 'buddy' to carry books and equipment between lessons
- Develop a strategy to use when fatigue is obvious – e.g. a designated quiet area for 10 minutes. The student probably does not need/may resent being asked to lie down or going to the quiet area for longer periods of time
- Reduce demands when appropriate – do not insist on continuation/completion of a task
- Discuss management of homework with staff, parents and student – is it necessary?
- Consider extra time in exams
- Reduce demands when appropriate

Epilepsy

- Obtain appropriate information regarding the nature of the student's epilepsy
- Find out if there is a dedicated epilepsy nurse at your local hospital to provide advice, or ask the school or college nurse

- When a student has a seizure, remain calm and do not over-react
- Follow published guidelines for managing seizures
- Ensure an area is available for the student to rest after seizures if necessary
- Keep a record of the times and duration of seizures and inform parents, if appropriate
- If a student with ABI shows unexpected inattention/daydreaming, inform his parent/s or discuss with the student if he is older and suggest it is mentioned at his next medical appointment
- If a student is taking anti-convulsant medication, report any increased tiredness, slowness or deterioration in academic work to his parents or discuss with the student if he is older, particularly if his medication has just been changed or increased

Language and communication

Word-finding difficulties

- Seek advice from a speech and language therapist for any aspect of language and communication difficulty
- If initial sound cues help, give these unless the student finds this embarrassing
- Prompt with whole words if this is acceptable to the student
- Ask the student to describe what he is attempting to name, if appropriate
- Provide a list of key words for specific topics
- Use multiple-choice assessment whenever possible

Language organisation difficulties

- Produce pro forma to structure work
- Provide headings, bullet points or key words
- Use software and other resources designed for dyslexics to aid organisation
- Support the student's communication efforts when speech is tangential, perseverative or rambling – e.g. use summarising comments or questions to redirect and focus

Slow language processing

- Provide as much information as possible in advance of lessons – e.g. next lesson we will be discussing volcanoes on page . . . of the textbook
- Allow as much extra time as possible for completion of work
- Repeat information in a different order and always recap information
- Whenever possible, provide short instructions or pieces of information interspersed by gaps
- Provide written backup for verbal information/instructions
- With the student's permission – if age appropriate, or permission from a young child's parents – alert other students to the need for patience and to allow longer response time

Language comprehension difficulties

- Simplify and rephrase instructions and information
- Provide verbal and written information in smaller amounts – 'chunking'
- Specifically teach skills to search for and extract information/meaning from text
- Provide any questions to be asked about it prior to the student reading text
- Assess his reading comprehension as well as his word recognition skills
- Provide a quiet environment at key times to encourage understanding of important information
- Ask the student to explain what he has been told in his own words to check his understanding
- Avoid use of sarcasm and other forms of irony
- Explain things directly – not by inference
- Provide summaries of complicated or obtuse text
- Encourage less language-based subjects when the student has curricular choice

Written language difficulties

- Allow alternative methods of recording – e.g. audio recordings, IT, etc.
- Highlight areas of the page that are ignored or confusing
- Reduce amounts to be read and provide some of the information verbally
- Present written information in small sections

- Place a piece of dark card over a page with a 'window' cut out so that the student can concentrate on just one part at a time
- Provide a quiet environment at key times to assist understanding of important information

Non-verbal communication difficulties

- Use video-interactive guidance for supporting these difficulties – trained practitioner required, following agreement from the parent/student

Attention

Sustained attention difficulties

- Use frequent changes of task whenever possible
- Allow brief breaks within a task
- Consider when important information is conveyed – try to ensure that this is at the beginning of a lesson or after a brief break, or that it is repeated at these times
- Give explicit instructions for what the student should be doing, avoiding commands such as 'pay attention'
- Be aware of 'attentional drift' and redirect the student – e.g. by making eye contact or saying his name before repeating relevant information
- Provide information in small, manageable chunks, avoiding information overload

Selective attention difficulties (distractibility)

- Allow quiet environments for specific, selected activities
- Reinforce specific information in a quiet environment if necessary
- Remove distractors from the immediate working environment – and remove the student if necessary, for instance, from windows with interesting views!
- Seek the student's undivided attention before speaking or instructing

Dividing attention difficulties

- Avoid the need for multi-tasking
- Give out handouts when information is being provided orally or when dictating
- Allow recording of orally presented information to enable note-taking at a later stage
- Allow the student to stop working when he is being spoken to or receiving further instructions – do not assume that he can, for instance, write and listen at the same time

Shifting attention difficulties

- Give advance warning of changes of activity whenever possible
- Allow 'settling down' time at the beginning of lessons
- Try not to provide important information or multi-tasked activities at the beginning of lessons, or if you do, then repeat it again later
- Repeat or prompt recall of information after a break

Memory

Working memory difficulties

- Provide prompt sheets and visual cues
- Categorise or group information or instructions to provide links – assist the student to learn this strategy
- Write down instructions, particularly multiple ones
- Use graphic or other visual organisers/aides-memoire for frequently required tasks/activities
- Encourage the student to request help or information when he is unsure what to do or doesn't understand

Long-term storage and recall difficulties

- Repetition, repetition, repetition! In different formats, situations, etc.
- Make information meaningful for the student

- Link new information to previously known facts and to topics of interest to the student
- Practise remembering; the need to recall information on a number of occasions – perhaps initially with a cue and then in response to an open-ended question – will assist encoding
- Use different modalities – e.g. multisensory work, as with dyslexics
- Provide cues to aid recall
- Use multiple-choice formats whenever possible
- Put questions in context and provide links with other information with which it was originally learnt
- Encourage use of memory aids – e.g. smartphone, diary, homework planner, list of key words, 'useful spellings', written summaries of key concepts, notes on class white board, etc.
- Use mnemonics and visualisation techniques
- Use flow charts and mind-mapping techniques

Verbal memory difficulties

- Use visual prompts and cues
- If appropriate to the student's age, explain visualisation techniques
- Whenever possible, use time lines, lists, flow charts, mind maps, graphs, pictures, drawings, photographs, PowerPoint presentations, tablet computers and printed handouts
- Encourage handwritten notes and prompts, checklists and calendars

Visual memory difficulties

- Use verbal and auditory inputs
- Record teaching sessions for the student to listen to later
- If appropriate, use reminder calls and messages
- If appropriate, use photographs of people, events or activities as prompts with verbal cues

Spatial memory difficulties

- If possible, keep the layout of teaching areas the same
- Warn of any necessary changes in advance

- Walk through any new routes or layouts with the student
- Use practical and visual ways to teach routes

Information processing

Slow information- and language-processing speed

- Allow more time for responses whenever possible
- Allow additional time to complete work
- Prompt when necessary – verbally or with provision of written/visual list – to reinforce set tasks
- Remember that significant amounts of information may have been missed
- Control amount of information that the student is to work with at any one time
- Set appropriate targets for quantity of work
- Modify expectations regarding homework and exams

Perception/sensation

Over-sensitivity to stimuli

- Seek advice from an occupational therapist
- Be aware of the student's difficulties and make allowances for extreme behavioural reactions to over-stimulation
- Inform peers of his difficulties as appropriate
- Arrange appropriate low-stimulus environments for times when concentration is particularly important

Other difficulties with sensory integration

- Seek advice from a specialist occupational therapist

Spatial skill difficulties

- Use pro forma or tables to assist setting out work
- Use very visible 'markers' in the physical environment
- Ensure safety in school or college and on outside visits

- Provide additional exercises with, for instance, positions and patterns
- Be aware of the difficulties and provide additional time/assistance when addressing relevant curricular areas – e.g. symmetry in Maths or work in Design Technology

Other visuo-perceptual difficulties

- Use books with clear, well-spaced text
- Provide additional work regarding matching, identification of shapes – including words – in pictures, text, the local environment, etc.
- Use a consistent format for important text
- Practice with visual, strategic searches
- Provide sorting activities – at any level
- Simplify visually presented material
- Highlight important information
- Use dark card or paper with 'windows' to reveal only small pieces of text at one time

Executive functioning

Planning and organising difficulties

- Assist the student to use a calendar or diary to list dates for work to be completed
- Provide extra assistance for time planning for older students
- Ask the student to compile a daily 'to do' list – with assistance, if necessary
- Use a daily planner and timetable
- Provide the first steps of a sequence for the student to complete
- Support the student to use visual organisers – e.g. step-by-step checklist of components of task or tasks for the student to cross off/remove/erase as completed
- Provide an uncluttered work area
- Limit the number of steps in a task
- Encourage the student to think of the next steps in a task – e.g. 'Good, now what will you do next?'
- Use 'advance organisers', i.e. information to help the student with a task prior to starting it – e.g. discuss and provide an outline of the task, key points, and purpose of the task

Problem-solving difficulties

- Reinforce problem solving in different curricular areas – e.g. What is the problem? What are ways of solving the problem? Think of several ways, plus pros and cons of each one; identify the best solution; create a plan of action; evaluate this
- Use problems that the student has experienced and discuss alternative strategies
- Encourage the student to think about alternatives and consequences
- Review completed tasks with the student – Could he have completed any parts more efficiently? Did he go off track/task at times? Did he repeat activities? etc.
- Use visual mapping techniques, if appropriate

Self-monitoring difficulties

- Use a 'traffic light' analogy and visual aid to help the student stop and think – 'Am I doing what I should be doing?'
- Teach the student to look for clues from others as to appropriateness of behaviour – e.g. 'reading' facial expressions that suggest disapproval
- Agree on a prompt to indicate inappropriate behaviour
- Encourage and assist self-reflection in older students – e.g. what behaviours made things better/worse?

Initiation difficulties

- Provide an agreed signal – which the student decides – to act as a reminder to start a task
- Have a very clear, visual and simple plan in the student's work area (e.g. Goal – Plan – Do)
- Incorporate a fun or novel element into stages of the task
- Provide steps of the task one at a time so as not to overwhelm the student
- Praise any attempt to initiate

Behaviour

- Provide structure – clear expectations, direction and organisation
- Have classroom rules prominently displayed, containing no more than five clear, concrete and positive statements, i.e. 'do' rather than 'don't'
- Involve students in the formulation of rules and discuss and explain these frequently
- Ensure that the students closest to the one with ABI are good models of behaviour
- Establish a format for the start and finish of each lesson – e.g. have an activity that students can get on with as soon as they enter the classroom, and have rules for leaving a classroom
- Redirect behaviour to a different topic or activity that is more acceptable – e.g. gain the student's attention and change the conversation, or direct the student to an activity with which he is already familiar and competent, one that does not require further explanations
- Keep level of stimulation low; be aware that bright lights, noise and a high activity level can create additional stress
- Establish clear routines – give notice of any changes
- Ensure the student has a clear timetable – time, location, activity and teacher's name if appropriate – to cover the whole day
- Provide choice and control whenever possible through acceptable choices towards an agreed upon goal – e.g. the order in which tasks are done, the materials used, etc.
- Follow a directed task with one which allows choice
- Be consistent. It is important for boundaries to be clearly stated and the same limits set by all members of staff
- Establish close proximity when the student is becoming anxious or excitable. Use the student's name and direct him back to task with a statement that will serve as a prompt/reminder about what he is meant to be doing
- Monitor the student frequently – breakdown of self-control can happen quickly, resulting in behaviour difficulties. Be sensitive to changes in his presentation
- Establish a regular format for cueing the student when giving information – e.g. by using his name. Ensure eye contact
- Provide verbal and visual directions. Use gestures as well as words, written and/ or pictorial information
- Ensure the student understands the task

- Model calm, controlled and predictable behaviour
- Provide clear statements that describe exactly what the desired behaviour is – e.g. 'Tom, please pick up your pen and continue to write your story about the invasion', rather than 'Tom, please behave yourself and get on'
- Be generous with approval of appropriate behaviour. Immediate feedback and reinforcement are important, so try to catch him behaving well and praise. State the specific behaviour that has been appropriate
- Expect variable performance and be prepared to modify expectations
- Help students to reflect on their own good behaviour – e.g. 'You sat quietly in the hall during assembly – that was great. What do you think about that?'

References

Blosser, J. L. and DePompei, R. (1994) 'Creating an effective classroom environment', in Savage, R. C. and Wolcott, G. F. (eds) *Educational Dimensions of Acquired Brain Injury*. Austin, TX: Pro-Ed, pp. 413–451.

Transitions

Returning to school is a series of transitions from the moment the student is injured until they graduate school and beyond, much like a chain that has a series of links tying itself together from beginning to end.

(Savage and Wolcott 1995)

Transitions imply change – change of class, change of year group, change of teacher, change of friends, change of school or college – which provoke alterations in expectations and responsibilities. Transitions are an inevitable part of life, part of the process of growing up and becoming more independent. Many people find change stressful and difficult to manage, but it is important to remember that any change – any transition – will be potentially more difficult and demanding for those with ABI than for many other students and may generate additional problems. Some of the most common transition times when particular difficulties can emerge are school and college transfers.

School and college transfers

Details relating to initial integration into school for a brain-injured preschooler or reintegration for an older student have been discussed in Chapter 5, and it is important to remember these same issues when students face transfer from one school to another or from one stage of learning to the next, including transfer to tertiary education.

Ability to cope with change

Students with cognitive difficulties following ABI frequently have problems coping with anything new, unexpected or different. They need consistent structure and routine. All young people benefit from this, but those with ABI can become more anxious, disorientated and fatigued in novel situations than their typically developing peers. They may react with inappropriate behaviour – challenging or withdrawn – and their school/college work may deteriorate. It is, therefore, very important that such changes are well planned in advance and that gradual familiarisation with the new environment and routine is built into a plan for such a transition. This applies to any plan for change, not just the Year 9 Transition Plan for those with Education, Health and Care Plans in England – the start of planning for the young person's transition to adulthood – although this is an ideal forum for good advance planning.

Impaired development and increasing demands

As young people increase in age, they normally develop skills to be able to complete greater amounts of more complex work more independently, and this is reflected in the demands of the curriculum and the learning environment. However, as has been discussed, those with acquired brain injuries often show impairment of that developmental trajectory years after their injury. It is not unusual to see a child who seemed to have been doing well in primary education suddenly present with a range of difficulties following transfer to secondary school. This can also sometimes be seen at the time of later transfers. Therefore, it is very important to consider potential problems in advance. Avoid assumptions that the student will cope, and give thought to the additional demands that may be made. Ensure that appropriate support is put in place to optimise success, before difficulties become apparent. If necessary, levels of support can be reduced at a later stage.

Many other students find increasing demands difficult and anxiety provoking, for instance when transferring to a much larger and very different environment in secondary education, and this has become a focus for additional support and guidance from both central government and local authorities in England in addition to publications produced by other organisations, e.g. the National Association for Special Educational Needs (NASEN) and the Transition Information Network provided by the Council for Disabled Children (see Useful organisations and resources). Such guidelines are not specifically written for those with ABI, but they can be relevant and helpful for those working with this population. They may need to be used selectively or with adaptations to take into account knowledge of the student's acquired deficits. For example, maps and photographs of a new environment are sometimes provided for young people to use as games prior to transfer to enable them to become familiar with the new setting. The young person with ABI may have any one of a number of cognitive or sensory difficulties that would make this approach inappropriate and, therefore, strategies need to be individually tailored to a student's needs.

Student involvement in transition planning

Student and family involvement in transition planning needs to be a priority. There must be plenty of opportunity for the student to be involved – to be at the centre of the process together with sufficient support. This is a form of person-centred planning and helps the student to become more independent, to be more in control of the transitions and changes that affect his life.

One-page profiles

Times of major transitions can be helped by the provision of one-page profiles, particularly for students with significant levels of need. These are simple summaries on one single sheet of paper or page of an electronic document, usually including a photo of the student, to show all that is important about them and how they want to be supported. The profiles commonly have three sections that the young person provides information about:

> 'What people appreciate about me'
> 'What's important to me'
> 'How best to support me'

One-page profiles provide a record that transitions with the student and can quickly assist staff in a new setting who may be unfamiliar with the student to recognise their strengths and personality as well as how best to provide support. Many websites explain the process and provide templates that can be downloaded, e.g. Helen Sanderson Associates (http://helensandersonassociates.co.uk/person-centred-practice/one-page-profiles/).

Transfer of information

Even if appropriate information is provided for a school or college and good planning takes place during initial reintegration, information is often not passed on when a student transfers to a new teacher, tutor group or setting. If support enables the student to do well, his underlying difficulties may be overlooked with the passage of time. Strategies can support the student to such an extent that it may seem they are no longer necessary. This assumption should never be made unless there has been a controlled reduction or removal of any such supports with a planned 'safety net'. Remember that, unfortunately, many of the problems caused by ABI cannot be 'cured', but it is possible to enable the student to learn to compensate for these. So, however well he seems to be doing, it is always important to pass on all relevant information and medical history to any new placement or set of teachers. There may be a need for training or awareness-raising for those who will subsequently be working with the young person. Continued assessment and monitoring remain essential. Partnership with parents is also vital and this is discussed in Chapter 12.

It is important that other professionals involved in planning transitions for the child or young person, such as personal careers advisers, have an awareness of issues relating to ABI in order to advise appropriately.

Prior to any change:

- begin planning well in advance
- review relevant information, records and current provision
- consider the demands of the new setting or situation
- arrange preliminary visits for familiarisation; obtain copies of timetables, lunch menus, list of clubs, etc.
- involve parents or other family members in the process
- anticipate any increased difficulties or demands the student may face
- plan how to address these
- put in place any additional necessary resources or support in advance
- arrange any necessary staff training
- identify a key member of staff for liaison
- pass on all relevant information and documentation to that person
- check if the key person has any queries after reading information about the student
- ensure there is an efficient system for disseminating relevant information to other staff members
- arrange a review soon after transfer to monitor provision and progress.

Transfer from school to college

Planning for transfer from school to college must take into account the complex issues provoked by ABI and the factors listed above. Colleges of Further Education can provide significant special needs support, but staff need detailed information about learning and behaviour needs if they are to do so effectively.

Young people with ABI who have been aware of the difficulties that they have faced in school are all too often heard to say that everything will be different once they transfer to college. They are frequently unaware of the nature or level of their own difficulties and can assume that these are related to the school environment. A realisation that the problems are exactly the same, or probably more evident, once they begin a college course can provoke a major reduction of self-esteem and subsequent failure to complete courses. Unfortunately, too many of these young people begin one or multiple courses which they then fail to complete and then end up staying at home with very low self-esteem – or even with developing mental health problems – unable to initiate educational, employment or social activities.

Some young people do not want information about their difficulties to be passed on to college staff. Sometimes they will express a wish to 'move on' and to 'make a fresh start'. This must be carefully and sensitively handled. Hopefully, if they have been well supported in school, encouraged to see the benefit of appropriate provision and become aware of their difficulties and strengths, then they may accept the need for transfer of information. However, if a young person remains resistant, then careful preparation work involving him and his parents will be necessary.

Some young people who have sustained severe brain injuries and who have a range of resultant difficulties may still be able to pursue courses of higher education, but once again, tutors must be made aware of their difficulties. Support for students with SEN and disabilities is also available at universities and provision can usually be put in place upon transfer of information. There may be the benefit of funds in England in the form of Disabled Students' Allowances. Following an assessment, these can provide additional resources for both under-graduate and post-graduate students. It is important to ensure that information about the young person's difficulties is transferred to new tutors in subsequent years or modules within the course. Examination dispensation should be sought where appropriate.

References

Savage, R. C. and Wolcott, G. F. (1995) *An Educator's Manual*. Washington, DC: Brain Injury Association Inc.

CHAPTER 12

Working with families

My child is not what she was, nor will she be what she was to become. Neither am I. Neither is anyone else in my family.

(Parent, in Savage and Morales 1996)

In 1989, David Hall, Consultant Paediatrician, wrote: 'Although one may empathise with parents who have a head injured child, it may be that only those who have been through such trauma can really understand'. It is important that we continue to recognise this and to understand its implications.

When the child or young person first becomes ill or suffers an injury, the family's world can be turned upside down. It may not be clear initially if he will survive and parents find themselves in an alien medical world, where they can feel powerless to do what they most wish to do – care for their child – and have to leave him in the hands of strangers. As detailed in Chapter 2, stages of early recovery can be unpredictable and frightening. Parents and other family members can find themselves on a roller coaster of emotional reactions.

In addition to fear, powerlessness and anxiety, issues of guilt and blame are common. This is sometimes referred to as survivor guilt. Occasionally, parents may be responsible for what has happened to their child, but more often than not the guilt is irrational. This does not make it less disabling. Parents naturally want to care for and to protect their children and so often feel responsible if anything happens to them. It can be difficult for them to avoid the many, 'If only . . .' questions. They may, of course, blame someone else – a car driver, the adult or sibling who was looking after the child, etc.

Brothers and sisters may also frequently feel guilt, particularly following a traumatic brain injury. This may be because they were present when their sibling was injured, or just because they are uninjured or have survived. It is not uncommon to find that siblings are secretly consumed by the idea that 'It should have been me'.

SIBLINGS OF CHILDREN WITH TBI. WHAT ABOUT THEM?

Question:

Our youngest daughter was hit by a swing more than two years ago in the playground. She was only 2 at the time. She sustained a severe TBI and has a lot of physical and cognitive issues that we are still working on in rehab. My question, though, is about her older brother who is now 6. He has become more withdrawn since his sister's injury. He used to be a very happy, outgoing little guy and now doesn't want to talk much or tell us what is bothering him. I can't tell if he feels guilty for some reason (he had nothing to do with her getting hurt though he was in the playground when it happened). And sometimes I think he might even be jealous of the constant attention that his sister gets, even though it's not the kind of attention a kid would ever want in the first place. We try our best to give him lots of attention and praise and involve him in activities he likes, but he seems to be falling deeper inside himself. What should we do?

Answer:

It is certainly perceptive that you have connected the changes in your son to your daughter's injury. As you already know, a serious brain injury affects everyone in the family. You and your spouse know the stress and strain you have lived through and no matter how much you have tried to shield your son, he, too, has felt these pressures.

You are absolutely right that he might feel both responsible and jealous. He was 4 years old when your daughter was injured – exactly the age when children can over-attribute others' behaviour to their own, and think that they have the ability to cause changes in the world. Four year olds can believe that their anger at a sister or brother could cause an accident. You've taken an important first step in recognizing this possible connection. The next step is to talk with your son about his feelings. Pick a quiet time when it's just the two of you and ask him if he even thinks about the accident. You can tell him directly that it wasn't his fault. Even though he saw it happen, he was only four and couldn't have prevented it. You can also let him know that feeling jealous is normal. It's okay to wish that sometimes he could have all the attention. You can talk with him about how your daughter's injury has affected the whole family.

Finally, consider several sessions for the whole family with a mental health therapist. This way, the spotlight would not be only on your son and he might feel more comfortable talking about his thoughts and feelings. And you might learn ways to help him regain his energy and optimism. He may require individual play-oriented therapeutic assessment to better understand his emotional needs if he is not able to articulate them.

(Gioia 2009 – copied with permission from Brainline.org)

If the child or young person remains in hospital for some time, additional strains are placed on the family. A parent may remain with their child in hospital and become totally involved in looking after him, to the exclusion of everything else. There can be significant disruption to family life – employment, finances, caring for other children and running the household can be difficult to concentrate on at this time. Immediate and extended family, friends and neighbours may provide important sources of practical and emotional support, but conversely, tensions can easily arise which can have a negative impact on relationships. The experiences of families following brain injury can be described in phases, from initial shock and disbelief, through times of adjustment, increasing aware-ness of the implications of the injury, to planning for the future with a member of the family who has dramatically changed needs. Klonoff (2014) provides such a model in seven phases that includes the impact of brain injury on different members of the family, and depending on their age/stage in life, different forms of psychological help that may be helpful for families in different situations and involving different forms of brain injury.

The role of the family has been frequently cited in the recovery process for young peo-ple with ABI. However, the care of the wider family is often overlooked, and their own needs may be neglected. Research indicates that families of young people with moderate to severe acquired brain injuries feel unsupported and isolated, and there is a desper-ate lack of and need for support from professional services (Gan et al. 2010; Jordan and Linden 2013). The consequences of acquired brain injury on behaviour, emotions and cognition are closely related to family distress and burden. The health and well-being of family members can severely deteriorate. High levels of stress and anxiety are experi-enced by parents of a young person with ABI on an ongoing basis (Hawley et al. 2003), and this can increase rather than decrease over time. Professional intervention may be needed for any or all family members even many years after the injury.

The resilience of families and how they coped prior to the injury is a good predictor of how they cope following the injury, but those with little or no support are more vulner-able. Families need help to build coping strategies, and to talk about any fears, anxieties and concerns they may have. There is an ongoing need for interventions and support that facilitate family adaptation.

Parents frequently say that they cannot wait for their child to be discharged from hospital and think that this will mark a turning point towards full recovery. Often young people do show a significant spurt in progress when they first return home and this encourages parents to hope for a full recovery.

> After hovering near death in a comatose state, this experience of reemergence was a powerful one . . . parents felt they had very strong emotional evidence to prove the worthiness of their undying hope. . . . Some parents did not understand that their child was forever changed until long after the accident.
>
> (Singer and Nixon 1996)

Sometimes, although parents do recognise many of the difficulties faced by their child and the differences in him, the full extent of these is only something that they may come to realise or to acknowledge over a long time. They have seen the remarkable progress that he has made from the time of his acute illness or injury. Why should they not believe that this will continue? In order to cope, they may only be able to accept or to understand a certain amount at any one time. Savage and Morales (1996) quote a parent who overheard a nurse saying that he was in 'denial'. He was well aware that he was in 'survival' rather than denial! It can be very easy for others to be judgemental regarding parents' reactions.

Everyone is unique in the way they respond to trauma and crisis. Some parents put huge amounts of energy into information gathering; some seek alternative therapies or treatments; some seek spiritual support or support from voluntary organisations; some refer to their child's difficulties frequently, others refuse to speak about them.

Whether or not they understand the full extent or impact of the young person's difficulties, it is nevertheless parents and other family members who do see changes. Frequently these are changes to the young person's personality and ability. They may appear subtle, or even nonexistent to others, but to the family, this person is different. Parents have lost a child that they knew. It is not surprising, therefore, that the reactions that this provokes are often compared with those seen when someone is bereaved. However, there are some crucial differences:

> The unique tragedy of brain injury, as compared to other terrible illnesses or accidents, is the loss of the person and their replacement by someone different. This new person is not totally different but is a pale shadow of the former self, a constant reminder of the lost child. Often it is the person's less desirable characteristics which are prominent. This situation is unlike the death of a child. The parents have no chance to finally accept and adjust; each day they have to deal with their grief again.
>
> (Hall 1989)

It is important not to ignore the continuing difficulties faced by siblings. They may be expected to take on additional responsibilities – to suddenly 'grow up' much more quickly and look after an older sibling. If the injured person's behaviour is unusual or inappropriate, this may be a cause of major embarrassment to his brothers and sisters. They may not want to be seen with him or to bring their friends home. They may feel unwanted or neglected, as their parents seem to be focusing on their injured brother. If usual family routines, activities or anticipated holidays are no longer possible, or changes are apparent within their parents' relationship, young people may become resentful and blame their injured sibling. Subsequent unhappiness, anxiety, depression or behavioural difficulties exhibited by their other children can, in turn, cause further anxiety for the parents.

As the young person so often seems to have made a good recovery, when he returns to education it can be the case that few problems are envisaged. Schools and colleges are frequently very positive in relation to the student's prospects and to his ability to address any apparent difficulties. Parents are frequently delighted that he is able to return to education and that the teachers are so encouraging.

However, many parents say that they then begin to realise that their child is facing difficulties and that these are not being recognised, but their concerns may be dismissed by members of staff. The most frequent comment heard from these parents regarding their child's teachers is, 'They just don't seem to understand!' Some parents give up trying to tell staff about their concerns at this stage, whereas others become increasingly vociferous and sometimes angry. School or college staff may then consider them to be overanxious or awkward.

Conversely, teachers sometimes report that parents expect too much of their child and refuse to accept his learning difficulties. This must be understood in the light of their previous aspirations based on his potential at that time and the difficulties inherent in accepting any changes to this.

Another issue that frequently causes disagreement or misunderstanding between parents and teachers is the effect of events or incidents reported by the student. As a result of the cognitive difficulties frequently faced by these students, their ability to accurately interpret situations or other people's actions may be impaired. It is relatively common for these students to go home and report, for instance, bullying by other students or unfair treatment by staff. There are, of course, times when this may be accurate, but there may also be times where this is not the case but is undoubtedly the young person's perception of events. Understandably, the parent often believes their child's version of events and, therefore, understanding and good communication are required to avoid conflicts or resentment.

It is of crucial importance that schools or colleges work with parents to meet the needs of a student. In order to do this effectively for a student with ABI, staff must have an understanding of the parents' situation and of the student's difficulties. There are some basic guidelines which are important to keep in mind:

- Recognise the nature and extent of the impact of the trauma on each and every member of the family.
- Always listen to what parents have to say. Never dismiss their opinions. They know their child better than anyone else.
- Avoid judgemental comments. Do not take criticism personally.
- Recognise why parents may find it hard to accept their child's limitations.
- Acknowledge and respect parental descriptions of the difficulties their child is encountering.

- Inform yourself about the possible effects of acquired brain injury.
- Maintain active and open communication with the student's parents. Seek their opinion and share information – remember they are partners in their child's education.
- Ask parents what strategies they find useful at home to address the student's difficulties.
- Be flexible.
- Avoid making assumptions.

It is interesting to note that some examples of schools or colleges where parents and staff have been seen to work closely together, ensuring that the student's needs have been well met, are those where staff have been very aware of or have witnessed the student's injury. This may be because the student was involved in a road traffic accident outside the school or college premises. Staff may have seen this happen; may have comforted other students and parents; may have seen paramedics working on the young person and may have watched an ambulance or air ambulance arrive. When staff have also been involved in some way in that initial trauma, they remain more conscious of the effects of this on the family. However, when a student enters a class or school looking well, perhaps years after his injury, members of staff do not have the benefit of that knowledge or memory. It is important that they take into account what the family has experienced.

Some of the best examples of educational provision designed to meet the needs of students with ABI have been planned in conjunction and co-operation with parents and with a flexible basis. When teachers do listen to parents, without preconceived ideas, they can often find ways of incorporating their ideas and suggestions to excellent effect. This is true partnership.

> Every step of the way for the past six and a half years, my wife and I have struggled to deal with people from a variety of professions who are ignorant of the complexities of acquired brain injury. From lawyers to medics to educationalists we have discovered that there is a serious lack of both knowledge and understanding. . . . Currently the child is expected to access their learning from within one of a small selection of boxes. This system is fundamentally flawed because it fails to recognise the specific individual requirements of the child. . . . A brain-injured child need not always become a disabled adult, dependent upon others for their very existence, but they do need to receive an education to enable them to reach their full potential.
>
> (Parent of a child with ABI)

References

Gan, C., Gargaro, J., Brandys, C., Gerber, G. and Boschen, K. (2010) 'Family caregivers' support needs after brain injury: A synthesis of perspectives from caregivers, programs and researchers'. *NeuroRehabilitation* 27 (1), pp. 5–18.

Gioia, G. A. (2009) Siblings of Children with TBI: What About Them? (www.brainline. org/content/2009/11/ask-the-expert-siblings-of-children-with-tbi-what-about-them. html).

Hall, D. (1989) 'Understanding parents', in Johnson, D. A., Uttley, D. and Wyke, M. (eds) *Children's Head Injury: Who Cares?* London: Taylor & Francis, pp. 171–182.

Hawley, C. A., Ward, A. B., Magnay, A. R. and Long, J. (2003) 'Parental stress and burden following traumatic brain injury amongst children and adolescents'. *Brain Injury* 17 (1), pp. 1–23.

Jordan, J. and Linden, M. (2013) 'It's like a problem that doesn't exist: The emotional well being of mothers caring for a child with brain injury'. *Brain Injury* 27 (9), pp. 1063–1072.

Klonoff, P. S. (2014) *Psychotherapy for Families after Brain Injury.* New York: Springer.

Savage, R. C. and Morales, K. J. (1996) 'The roller coaster: The changing roles of the family in the ongoing recovery of their child', in Singer, G. H. S., Glang, A. and Williams, J. M. (eds) *Children with Acquired Brain Injury: Educating and Supporting Families.* Baltimore, MD: Paul H. Brookes, pp. 65–78.

Singer, G. H. S. and Nixon, C. (1996) 'A report on the concerns of parents of children with ABI', in Singer, G. H. S., Glang, A. and Williams, J. M. (eds) *Children with Acquired Brain Injury: Educating and Supporting Families.* Baltimore, MD: Paul H. Brookes, pp. 23–52.

Mild traumatic brain injury (and sports concussion)

No head injury is too severe to despair of nor too trivial to ignore.

(Translation from Hippocrates, fourth century BC)

There is now much more awareness of the potential consequences of mild traumatic brain injuries (mTBI) and this has come about particularly as a result of focus on those that occur during sporting activities, often referred to as sports-related concussions – in some of the literature, just the term 'concussion' is used as an alternative to mTBI.

Most people who have sustained an mTBI or concussion make a full recovery relatively quickly, but there is now an awareness that mild injuries can cause long-lasting effects. There has been a significant amount of recent research regarding these effects and their causes. It has been of concern to those who study the effects of trauma to the brain that minor concussion has often been discounted by many as trivial, without consideration of possible effects. There is also awareness of the importance of strategies that must always be applied following a concussion in order to minimise the risk of ongoing symptoms.

As long ago as 1993, a definition of mTBI was developed by the American Congress of Rehabilitative Medicine (ACRM), but it is only the recent research that has led scientists and clinicians to produce specific protocols, particularly for injuries to young people and adults on the sports field. These are relevant to those working within education. Although the checklists refer specifically to sports injuries, consideration of these can raise awareness in families and educators regarding symptoms following any concussion, and precautions that should be taken. The widely available 'recognition tools' that can be used by non-medical professionals are endorsed by sporting bodies, such as the RFU (England Rugby), FA (Football Association), FIFA (Fédération Internationale de Football Association), FEI (Fédération Equestre Internationale), IRB (World Rugby), etc. In addition to checklists for the presence of concussion and recommendations for seeking medical attention, there are also strict guidelines relating to return to play and to training. The checklist approved and issued by the above organisations is included at the end of this chapter.

It is of note from this checklist that a person who suffers an mTBI may or may not be rendered unconscious – and then for no longer than 30 minutes or the injury would then not be considered 'mild' – and also that the presence of only one of the symptoms listed can indicate a brain injury, including feeling 'dazed'.

This is important, because the largest proportion of traumatic brain injuries sustained by children and young people can be classified as mild and many of those who sustain minor concussions may never even be referred to a doctor. Despite the probable even greater numbers who are not seen by a medical professional, it has been reported that over half a million children and adolescents present to emergency departments in the United States each year with mTBI (Faul et al. 2010).

The effects of an mTBI or concussion – often referred to as post-concussive symptoms – commonly include symptoms such as dizziness, headache, slowed visual motor speed and reaction time and impaired sleep patterns, in addition to cognitive issues such as reduced attentional, information processing and working memory ability. The young person may also demonstrate frustration or anxiety relating to these symptoms and possible irritability. Most of these symptoms in children and young people will generally resolve within one to two weeks (Brooks et al. 2014; Lax et al. 2015). However, it is recognised that, even within this relatively brief time, if these symptoms are not acknowledged and too many demands are made of the young person, particularly in educational or physical exercise environments, then the symptoms may be exacerbated. In 2015, a leading expert in the field noted:

> When considering the clinical needs of the student with a concussion in the academic context, there are two primary targets for management: the effect of the concussion on school learning and performance and the effect of school learning and performance on concussion recovery.
>
> (Gioia 2015; citing Sady et al. 2011)

During the time that the student is recovering from the effects of the mTBI, he may be suffering from any or all of the above symptoms that may well affect his ability and performance in the classroom. Studies have shown that cognitive exertion may provoke an increase in post-concussion symptoms (e.g. Gioia et al. 2011). The most effective way to promote a speedy and full recovery is to ensure that physical and cognitive demands are temporarily reduced in line with the student's capabilities at that time. If this does not happen, the effects may exacerbate or extend. However, despite appropriate intervention, symptoms may persist for a small number of young people.

One reason that it is important to be vigilant and to monitor any young person who has sustained an mTBI or sports-related concussion is because of difficulties that may occur in diagnosis. Even if a young person is seen in a hospital setting, it may not be possible initially to diagnose the severity of a concussive injury, nor its potential to provoke continuing symptoms (Brooks et al. 2014), and such injuries are usually not visible even on brain scans (Rhine et al. 2016). Education professionals and parents must consult together to make judgements regarding the timing of return to previous academic pro-grammes and consult medical professionals if there are any ongoing concerns. Research indicates that cognitive difficulties may endure longer than other symptoms of which the young person might be aware and report, such as their head hurting or feeling dizzy. Apart from during the first 24 hours, there are indications that, for many young people, total rest may not be helpful during this recovery period and that optimum progress may be made with a continuation of moderate levels of activity (Majerske et al. 2008), but it is important to seek advice from an appropriately qualified medical professional.

Young people with developing brains are more susceptible to the effects of concus-sive injuries than adults (Field and Dolske 2007). Even if recoveries follow what can appear to be a 'normal' trajectory, young people frequently take longer to recover than adults. There are also indications that there may be differences in recovery patterns depending on the age of the child or adolescent. Some researchers have suggested that girls are more susceptible to the effects of mTBI in contact sports or to sustaining such an injury than their male counterparts (e.g. Covassin and Elbin 2011; Broshek et al. 2005). Research regarding this is ongoing, but in 2012 the American Medical Society for Sports Medicine issued a position statement which said: 'recent data shows with sports with similar rules female athletes sustain more concussions than male counterparts. Female athletes report a higher number and severity of symptoms and longer duration of recovery than male counterparts' (Harman et al. 2013).

The clear indications from all this are that advice should be given to young people and their families following such an injury. Education staff should be aware, supportive and knowledgeable regarding the possible effects of injuries and their management. This includes the risk of a reduction in academic ability and physical stamina for at least a short time following a concussion (Gioia 2015).

As so many concussive injuries are sustained during sporting activities, another major issue for young people relates to when they should be allowed to return to play. This can be affected by coaches or teachers not wanting to lose good sportspeople or team mem-bers and that keen young sportspeople may also minimise or ignore symptoms in their enthusiasm to return to play. Education that raises awareness about concussion can help to counteract this problem.

In a forward to a special edition of the journal *Brain Injury* dedicated to sports concus-sion, Barth and Broshek (2015) stated:

> sports concussion has become one of the signature public health issues of the time. Profes-sional sports garner the most attention in the public discourse on concussion, but sports participation is a part of the fabric of child development, education and health and the threat of neurologic injury in youth and the potential long-term sequelae has generated a level of concern that has mobilized the general public to join the debate and to seek answers.

Awareness of this issue in the USA has risen to the extent that President Obama hosted a 'Healthy Kids and Safe Sports Concussion Summit' in the White House in 2014, and there are education programmes and state legislation relating to concussion management in education settings across that country.

There is also considerable evidence to indicate the risks of multiple concussive injuries, particularly if these occur when the young person has not fully recovered from a previous one. A study of adolescent rugby players concluded that it is important to differentiate between outcomes following mTBI as a one-off event and those sustained in collision sports where there can be an expectation of a more pronounced cumulative effect (Alexander et al. 2015). This is the reason for the emergence of revised guidelines and protocols regarding return to play in contact sports. All these recommend a conservative approach when working with children and adolescents who have sustained sports concussions with a very gradual and closely monitored return to slowly increasing levels of activity prior to return to the field of play. The US Centers for Disease Control and Prevention (CDC) provides information online under its Heads Up programme (www.cdc.gov/headsup).

Sports concussion checklist

This checklist has been approved by many national and international sporting federations. It was devised for adolescents and adults so some of the terminology is developmentally inappropriate for younger children. The symptoms and questions are therefore not all relevant or may need adjusting to suit the situation and the age of the young person. However, it is included as it may help to increase awareness of a wide range of possible effects following an mTBI.

Concussion should be suspected if one or more of the following visible clues, signs and symptoms or errors in memory questions are present.

1) *Visible clues of a suspected concussion*
     Any one or more of the following visual clues can indicate a possible concussion:
        Loss of consciousness or responsiveness
        Lying motionless on ground/slow to get up
        Unsteady on feet/balance problems or falling over/incoordination
        Grabbing/clutching at head
        Dazed, blank or vacant look
        Confused/not aware of plays/events

2) *Signs and symptoms of suspected concussion*
     Presence of any one or more of the following signs and symptoms may suggest a concussion:

Loss of consciousness	*Headache*
Seizure or convulsion	*Dizziness*
Balance problems	*Confusion*
Nausea or vomiting	*Feeling slowed down*
Drowsiness	*"Pressure in head"*

More emotional	Blurred vision
Irritability	Sensitivity to light
Sadness	Amnesia
Fatigue or low energy	Feeling like "in a fog"
Nervous or anxious	Neck pain
Don't feel right	Sensitivity to noise
Difficulty remembering	Difficulty concentrating

3) **Memory function**

Failure to answer any of these questions correctly may suggest a concussion:

What venue are we at today?

Which half is it now?

Who scored last in this game?

What team did you play for last week/game?

Did your team win the last game?

Any athlete with a suspected concussion should be IMMEDIATELY REMOVED FROM PLAY, and should not be returned to activity until they are assessed medically. Athletes with a suspected concussion should not be left alone and should not drive a motor vehicle.

It is recommended that, in all cases of suspected concussion, the player is referred to a medical professional for diagnosis and guidance as well as return to play decisions, even if the symptoms resolve.

Red flags

If ANY of the following are reported then the player should be safely and immediately removed from the field. If no qualified medical professional is available, consider transporting by ambulance for urgent medical assessment:

Athlete complains of neck pain	Deteriorating conscious state
Increasing confusion or irritability	Severe or increasing headache
Repeated vomiting	Unusual behaviour change
Seizures or convulsions	Double vision
Weakness or tingling/burning in arms or legs	

References

Alexander, D. G., Shuttleworth-Edwards, A. B., Kidd, M. and Malcolm, C. M. (2015) 'Mild traumatic brain injuries in early adolescent rugby players: Long term neurocognitive and academic outcomes'. *Brain Injury* 29 (9), pp. 1113–1125.

Barth, J. T. and Broshek, D. K. (2015) 'Forward'. *Brain Injury: Special Edition on Sports Concussion* 29 (2), pp. 127–128.

Brooks, B. L., Khan, S., Daya, H., Mikrogianakis, A. and Barlow, K. M. (2014) 'Neurocognition in the emergency department after a mild traumatic brain injury in youth'. *Journal of Neurotrauma* 31, pp. 1744–1749.

Broshek, D. K., Kaushik, T., Freeman, J. R., Erlanger, D., Webbe, F. and Barth, J. T. (2005) 'Sex differences in outcome following sports-related concussion'. *Journal of Neurosurgery* 102 (5), pp. 856–863.

Covassin, T. and Elbin, R. J. (2011) 'The female athlete: The role of gender in the assessment and management of sport-related concussion'. *Clinics in Sports Medicine* 30 (1), pp. 125–131.

Faul, M., Xu, L., Wald, M. W. and Coronado, V. G. (2010) 'Traumatic brain injury in the United States: Emergency department visits, hospitalizations, and deaths 2002–2006'. Atlanta, GA: Centers for Disease Control and Prevention, National Center for Injury Prevention and Control.

Field, M. and Dolske, M. (2007) 'Pathophysiology of sports concussion: Are kids different?'. *Brain Injury Professional* 4 (4), pp. 20–21.

Gioia, G. A. (2015) 'Multimodal evaluation and management of children with concussion: Using our heads and available evidence'. *Brain Injury* 29 (2), pp. 195–206.

Gioia, G. A., Gerst, E., McGuire, E., McGill, C., Palacias, M. and Vaughan, C. (2011) 'Standardized assessment of cognitive exertion effects in paediatric mild TBI: Application of reliable change methodology'. *Journal of the International Neuropsychological Society* 17, p. 134.

Harman, K. G., Drezner, J., Gammons, M., Guskiewicz, K., Halstead, M., Herring, S., Kutcher, J., Pana, A., Putukian, M. and Roberts, W. (2013) 'American medical society for sports medicine position statement: Concussion in sport'. *Clinical Journal of Sport Medicine* 1, pp. 1–18.

Lax, I. D., Pannicia, M., Agnihotris, S., Reed, N., Garmaise, E., Azadbakhsh, M., Ng, J., Manette, G., Wisement-Hakes, C., Taha, T. and Keightley, M. (2015) 'Development and gender influences on executive function following concussion in youth hockey players'. *Brain Injury* 29 (12), pp. 1409–1419.

Majerske, C. W., Mihalik, J. P., Ren, D., Collins, M. W., Reddy, C. C., Lovell, M. R. and Wagner, A. K. (2008) 'Concussion in sports: Postconcussive activity levels, symptoms, and neurocognitive performance'. *Journal of Athletic Training* 43, pp. 265–274.

Rhine, T., Babcock, L., Zhang, N., Leach, J. and Wade, S. (2016) 'Are UCH-L1 and GFAP promising biomarkers for children with mild traumatic brain injury'. *Brain Injury* 30 (10), pp. 1231–1238.

Sady, M. D., Vaughan, C. G. and Gioia, G. A. (2011) 'School and the concussed youth: Recommendations for concussion education and management'. *Physical Medicine and Rehabilitation Clinics of North America* 22, pp. 701–719.

Useful organisations and resources

All of the websites below were operational at the time of going to press. However, the precise addresses of websites can be unreliable due to pages and related documents being updated, reorganised, or even disappearing altogether. If this happens, try typing key words into a search engine.

Education

ACE Education Advice & ACE Education Training www.ace-ed.org.uk Independent organisation for parents and educators providing information, training and consultancy relating to all aspects of education. Advice line: 0300 0115142

Department for Education (DfE) provides a number of downloadable resources:

The Special Educational Needs and Disabilities (SEND) code of practice: 0 to 25 years is at www.gov.uk/government/publications/send-code-of-practice-0-to-25

The SEND guide for parents and carers is at www.gov.uk/government/publications/send-guide-for-parents-and-carers

Keeping children safe in education: statutory guidance for schools and colleges is at www.gov.uk/government/uploads/system/uploads/attachment_data/file/550511/keeping_children_safe_in_education.pdf

Supporting pupils at school with medical conditions: statutory guidance for governing bodies of maintained schools and proprietors of academies in England is at www.gov.uk/government/publications/supporting-pupils-at-school-with-medical-conditions-3

Mental Health and Behaviour in Schools: Departmental advice for school staff is at www.gov.uk/government/uploads/system/uploads/attachment_data/file/508847/Mental_Health_and_Behaviour_-_advice_for_Schools_160316.pdf

Enchanted Learning www.enchantedlearning.com Provides easy to read information about the brain and a few suggested classroom activities.

First Tier Tribunal (Special Educational Needs and Disability) www.gov.uk/courts-tribunals/first-tier-tribunal-special-educational-needs-and-disability/about To appeal against an Education, Health and Care (EHC) plan decision or to complain about disability discrimination.

Home Education and Special Needs England http://ehe-sen.org.uk Web-based information for parents who choose to home educate children with special needs.

Independent Parental Special Education Advice (IPSEA) www.ipsea.org.uk Provides free and independent legally based information, advice and support for parents of students with special educational needs. Offers access to a mailing list; an advice line; tribunal helpline; and general information service. Tribunal helpline: 01799 582030

Joint Council for Qualifications www.jcq.org.uk Publishes a document of regulations and guidance relating to examination candidates with particular requirements, giving details of arrangements and allowances made each year for candidates who require something different from the standard arrangements for assessment (access arrangements and reasonable adjustments), e.g. extra time, amanuensis, etc.

National Society for Special Educational Needs (NASEN) www.nasen.org.uk Promotes the advancement and development of all individuals with SEND/ALN, and produces journals, policy documents and other publications on a range of special educational issues.

Network 81 www.network81.org.uk Supports, advises and trains parents and carers about the education of children with special educational needs and disabilities. Helpline: 0845 077 4055

Neuroscience for Kids http://faculty.washington.edu/chudler/neurok.html A website dedicated to providing information for students and teachers who want to learn more about the brain and spinal cord. It includes a range of activities such as games, model making, etc.

Parents for Inclusion www.parentsforinclusion.org A national charity run by parents for parents. Provides advocacy, support, education and training.

Project LEARNET (US site) www.projectlearnet.org Resource for teachers, clinicians, parents and students by the Brain Injury Association of New York State. Includes a problem-solving system to identify methods of support for students with ABI.

Rathbone www.rathboneuk.org A charitable organisation providing a range of courses across the UK and specialist provision for 14+ year-olds who have been partially or fully excluded from school.

United Kingdom Council for Child Internet Safety (UKCCIS) www.gov.uk/government/groups/uk-council-for-child-internet-safety-ukccis A group of more than 200 organisations that work in partnership to help keep children safe online. Advice for schools and colleges, sexting in schools and colleges, responding to incidents and safeguarding young people.

Health

Adders www.adders.org Provides information for raising awareness about ADD and ADHD, together with practical advice.

Kids Health www.kidshealth.org A jargon-free health information site that has separate areas of age-appropriate content for children, teenagers, educators and parents.

MindEd www.minded.org.uk Web-based mental health resource for adults working with or caring for children and young people. Funded by the Department for Education and accredited by the NHS Information Standard.

Sensory Integration Network www.sinetwork.org

Young Minds www.youngminds.org.uk A children's mental health charity which offers a range of information and materials on mental health issues. Parents helpline: 0808 802 5544

Counselling

The British Association for Counselling and Psychotherapy (BACP) www.bacp.co.uk The professional body in the UK that sets and monitors practice and standards in counselling and psychotherapy.

British Association of Play Therapists www.bapt.info/bapt/ Information about Play Therapy and how to find therapists.

Place2Be www.place2be.org.uk National mental health charity. Provides in-school emotional and therapeutic services for both primary and secondary age ranges. Tel: 020 7923 5500

Young Minds http://youngminds.org.uk Charity committed to improve the well-being and mental health of children and young people. Parents' helpline: 0808 802 5544

Disability rights

Equality and Human Rights Commission www.equalityhumanrights.com Provides advice and information for parents and schools, outlining rights and equality of access.
Inclusive Solutions www.inclusive-solutions.com Provides information about techniques to consider for group work that promotes social/emotional skills.

General behaviour difficulties

DfE document https://www.gov.uk/government/publications/behaviour-in-schools Creating a Culture: How school leaders can optimise behaviour. An independent review.

Sexual behaviour

The Family Planning Association www.fpa.org.uk Offers a range of pamphlets, books, resource packs and videos on sexual matters. There is advice for parents and a wide range of resources for them to use with children who have learning difficulties.

Bullying

Anti-Bullying Alliance www.anti-bullyingalliance.org.uk/media/5436/Mental-health-and-bullying-module-FINAL.pdf Bullying and mental health: guidance for teachers and other professionals.

Other organisations relevant for those with ABI, their teachers and families

AFASIC www.afasic.org.uk Information and training to support young people with speech, language and communication impairments. Parents' helpline: 0300 666 9410

Affinity Hub www.affinityhub.uk Emotional support for parents of children with special needs.

ARCOS (Association for Rehabilitation of Communication and Oral Skills) www.arcos.org.uk Supports children and adults with communication and/or swallowing problems from developmental or acquired brain injury.

Ataxia UK www.ataxia.org.uk Support groups and information plus specific group for young people from 16 years of age. Helpline: 0845 644 0606

Brain Injury Hub www.braininjuryhub.co.uk Created by The Children's Trust. ABI information for children and families/carers, plus forums, news and blogs.

Brain and Spine Foundation www.brainandspine.org.uk Information, support and a discussion forum. Helpline: 0808 808 1000

Brain and Spine Injury Charity (BASIC) www.basiccharity.org.uk Counselling, rehabilitation and support for those with brain injuries. Support for families and carers. Helpline: 0870 750 0000

The Brain Tumour Charity www.thebraintumourcharity.org Information and support, and dedicated children's and families service. Information and activities for children and families and organised family days, plus HeadSmart campaign to reduce diagnosis times for childhood brain tumours.

Child Brain Injury Trust www.childbraininjurytrust.org.uk Information, support, learning events and specific Youth Zone in the website. Helpline: 0303 303 2248

Children's Hemiplegia and Stroke Association (US based) www.chasa.org Wide range of information and linked email discussion group for parents and children at www.hemikids.org.

The Children's Trust www.thechildrenstrust.org.uk Residential and community services for children and young people with acquired brain injury. School, family, education and care support.

Contact-a-Family www.cafamily.org.uk Support for families of all children with a disability. Helpline: 0808 808 3555

Different Strokes www.differentstrokes.co.uk Support for younger stroke survivors.

The Encephalitis Society www.encephalitis.info Support and information for individuals affected by encephalitis, their families and for professionals. Helpline: 01653 699599

Epilepsy Action www.epilepsy.org.uk Support and information for children and adults. Training for school staff and other professionals. Helpline: 0808 800 5050

Epilepsy Society www.epilepsysociety.org.uk Information, training, diagnosis and treatment, specialist care services. Helpline: 01494 601 400

Headway, the brain injury association www.headway.org.uk Services and information for brain injury survivors, their families and carers and for professionals. Helpline: 0808 800 2244

Hemihelp www.hemihelp.org.uk Information, support and guidance for those with hemiplegia and their families.

I Can – the children's communication charity www.ican.org.uk Information, help and advice for parents and practitioners about speech, language and communication, plus assessment services.

Meningitis Now www.meningitisnow.org Information and support for those with meningitis and their families. Helpline: 0808 8010 388

National Children's Bureau www.ncb.org.uk/resources-publications Provides fact sheets and information on a wide range of issues relating to education and care.

National Tremor Foundation www.tremor.org.uk Information and support.

Shine (Spina bifida, Hydrocephalus, Information, Networking, Equality) www.shinecharity.org.uk Support for individuals, families and professionals.

Stroke Association www.stroke.org.uk Provides information and support and detailed guidelines, for instance for parents/carers of children affected by stroke. Helpline: 0303 3033

Young Epilepsy www.youngepilepsy.org.uk Information and support for parents. Information, resources and training courses for professionals in health, social care and education, plus promotion of good practice in schools. Helpline: 01342 831342

Safety and injury prevention

Cycle-smart Foundation www.cycle-smart.org Promotes safer cycling and, in particular, use of cycling helmets. Provides educational material for use in schools with children of different ages.

Child Accident Prevention Trust www.capt.org.uk Child safety advice for parents/carers and professionals working with children and families.

ThinkFirst, National Injury Prevention Foundation (US-based) www.thinkfirst.org Programmes for students for use in schools and other settings to raise awareness on preventing traumatic injuries, particularly of the brain and spinal cord.

Glossary

Absences: a type of epileptic seizure previously known as petit mal. The person loses consciousness only briefly, becoming 'blank' and unresponsive for just a few seconds, so the seizures may go unnoticed

Acceleration/deceleration injury: injury to the brain caused when it is moving at speed (e.g. in a vehicle) and then abruptly stops – e.g. in a road traffic accident. The head does not strike anything

Amnesia: lack of memory about events occurring during a particular period of time

Aneurism: a deformity in the wall of a blood vessel which can cause it to bulge like a balloon. If this bursts, it provokes a haemorrhage

Ankle foot orthosis (AFO): a moulded brace that stabilises the ankle joint

Anoxia: lack of oxygen to the brain

Anti-convulsants: medication to prevent or reduce seizures

Aphasia: an inability to communicate with – and sometimes to understand – language

Ataxia: movements characterised by incoordination, tremor or both and caused by damage to the brain. Ataxia can affect fine motor skills, gross motor skills and speech

Axons: the usually long and straight part of a neuron or nerve cell that conducts impulses – messages – away from the cell body to another neuron

Bilateral: referring to both sides of the body

Brainstem: the lower extension of the brain where it connects to the spinal cord. Survival – breathing, heart rate – and arousal – being awake and alert – functions are located in the brainstem

Central nervous system (CNS): the brain and spinal cord

Cerebellum: part of the brain located at the back, below the cortex, that relates particularly to movement – damage to this area can provoke ataxia

Cerebral cortex: the outer part of the brain, made up of two hemispheres, each with four lobes – frontal, temporal, parietal, occipital

Cerebrospinal fluid (CSF): a colourless fluid that is produced in the brain and fills the space in the brain called the ventricles. It circulates around the brain and spinal cord

Closed head/brain injury: one type of traumatic brain injury. In this type of injury, the skull is not penetrated. It is the most common type of injury and often occurs from road traffic accidents, falls, or shaking in babies

Cognition: the processes involved in thinking, learning, knowing and problem solving

Coma: a state of unconsciousness following injury to the brain from which the person cannot be roused, characterised by lack of voluntary eye opening, response to simple commands or comprehensible speech

Computerised tomography (CT) or computerised axial tomography (CAT): scans involving a series of images taken at different levels of the brain – or other parts of the body

Concussion: an alteration of consciousness caused by an injury to the brain – usually a blow to the head

Confabulation: to elaborate speech or fill in gaps in memory with information that has no base in reality

Contrecoup: the word coup in French means strike or blow. Contrecoup refers to an injury at the opposite side of the brain to the original impact, when the brain rebounds within the skull

Contusion: bruise

Corpus callosum: a band of fibres that connects the two hemispheres of the brain and enables rapid communication between them

Cyst: an abnormal sac or cavity filled with liquid or semi-solid matter

Dendrites: 'branches' extending from neurons or nerve cells that carry incoming signals into the cell

Diffuse axonal injury: widespread injury to the brain caused by shearing – tearing – of axons as a result of acceleration/deceleration injuries, such as in a road traffic accident

Diplopia: seeing two images of a single object – double vision

Disinhibition: inability to suppress impulsive speech or actions

Dysarthria: a motor speech disorder caused by weakness, slowness or incoordination of the muscles involved in speech. The severity can range from no ability to produce intelligible speech to a mild articulation difficulty

Dysphasia: impaired ability to communicate with and/or to understand language

Dyspraxia: impaired ability to plan and execute co-ordinated or sequenced movements

Echolalia: repetition of words or speech sounds without comprehension or meaning as communication

EEG (electroencephalogram): the trace of a recording of electrical activity in different parts of the brain

Emotional lability: sudden changes or extreme reactions of emotional state

Encephalopathy: any of various diseases that affect the functioning of the brain

Epilepsy: a group of disorders of brain function, due to uncoordinated electrical activity, that are characterised by recurrent attacks with sudden onset

Executive functions: include the ability to set goals, plan and strategically problem-solve, initiate actions, inhibit inappropriate responses and monitor or control behaviour. The frontal lobes are mainly responsible for executive functions, but other areas of the brain are also involved

Fine motor skills: small physical actions such as those made by the hands, fingers and toes

Focal brain injury: an injury solely to a specific area of the brain – rare in traumatic brain injury

Frontal lobes: the part of the brain at the front – left and right. This area of the brain plays a role in controlling emotions, motivation, social skills, expressive language, inhibition of impulses, planning, organising, problem solving, and higher-level cognitive – or executive – skills

Gait: walking pattern

Glasgow Coma Scale (GCS): a frequently used scale to help towards assessing the severity of a brain injury, based on three components of consciousness: eye opening, verbal response and motor response. The scale is on a range of 3–15: a mild brain injury is usually thought to correspond to a score of 13–15, a moderate injury to a score of 9–12, and a severe injury to a score of 3–8. The lowest possible coma score is 3. There is a modified version for children too young to have reliable language skills.

Glial cells: the most abundant cells in the brain. As it was initially thought that they just hold the structure together, they were named glial – meaning 'glue'. However, there are different types of glial cells and their functions are complex: they support and protect the neurons and are important in forming and maintaining connections

Gross motor skills: actions performed by large muscle groups – i.e. major body movements

Haematoma: a collection of blood within tissue that then clots

Haemorrhage: the escape of blood from a ruptured blood vessel

Hemianopia: an inability to see within one half of the visual field

Hemiparesis: a weakness – affecting movement or use of limbs – on one side of the body

Hemiplegia: a degree of paralysis of limbs on one side of the body

Hemisphere: one half of the brain – either left or right

Hydrocephalus: an abnormal increase in the amount of cerebrospinal fluid in the ventricles of the brain, causing increased intracranial pressure

Hypoxia: insufficient oxygen supply to tissues of the body

Intracranial pressure: the pressure level within the skull, altered by swelling of tissue or increase in amount of cerebrospinal fluid

Ischaemia: an inadequate flow of blood to a part of the body, caused by constriction or blockage of the blood vessels supplying it

Lesion: an abnormality of or damage to tissue in the body, caused by disease or trauma

Limbic system: area at the upper end of the brainstem that contains structures relating, among other things, to emotion and memory

Magnetic resonance imaging (MRI): a computer imaging technique that produces more detailed scans to generate images of the internal structure of the brain

Meninges: three protective layers covering the brain and spinal cord

Metacognition: insight into strengths and weaknesses with regard to learning-cognition – or knowing how you learn

Motor control: Fine – co-ordination of muscles to make intricate movements, particularly involving the hands; **Gross** – co-ordination of muscles to make large body movements

Myelin: insulating material that gradually forms a sheath around axons

Neonatal: the time from birth up to 6 weeks old

Neural networks: neurons that connect together using electrical or chemical signals to form a 'network'

Neurologist: a doctor who specialises in disorders that affect the brain and spinal cord and the nerves that connect these to every other part of the body

Neuron: a nerve cell within the brain

Neuropsychologist: a psychologist who specialises in the cognitive and behavioural changes related to brain abnormalities. A paediatric neuropsychologist specialises in the problems of children with brain disorders

Occipital lobe: the posterior section of each hemisphere of the brain, including areas responsible for interpretation of visual images

Oedema: excess build-up of fluid in body tissue, often causing swelling

Open head/brain injury: a type of brain injury where the skull is penetrated and the underlying brain exposed

Parietal lobe: the upper middle part of each side of the brain, behind the frontal lobes. Responsible, for instance, for visuo-spatial skills – right hemisphere – and some language functions – usually left hemisphere

Perseveration: inappropriate repetition of actions, thoughts or speech

Post-traumatic amnesia (PTA): a time following a brain injury when a person does not have reliable continuous memory for day-to-day events. This is a good indicator of severity of injury, but can be difficult to assess in young children

Pragmatics: use of language in social contexts and understanding meaning beyond the literal

Premorbid: prior to onset of illness or injury

Proprioception: awareness of the position of parts of the body without visual feedback – e.g. knowing where your hand is and being able to touch it with the other without looking

Psychometric assessments: standardised tests to assess cognitive functioning

Quadriparesis: weakness of all four limbs

Quadriplegia: a degree of paralysis of all four limbs – sometimes termed tetraplegia

Rancho Los Amigos Scale of Cognitive Functions: a measure of the stages of recovery following a brain injury

Reinforcement: any consequence that increases the likelihood of the occurrence of a particular behaviour

Retrograde amnesia: an inability to remember information from a specific length of time prior to a brain injury – e.g. minutes to months

Seizures: commonly known as 'fits', temporary 'attacks' with or without a loss of consciousness and caused by abnormal electrical activity in the brain as a result of epilepsy or trauma

Shunt: in this context, a valve and tube surgically inserted to drain excess cerebrospinal fluid from the brain to the chest or abdominal cavity

Spasticity: causes an involuntary increase in muscle tone when limbs are moved, provoking resistance. Caused by brain or spinal cord damage

Stroke: an interruption of the blood flow to the brain, caused by a blockage due to a blood clot – ischaemic stroke – or if a weakened blood vessel ruptures and bleeds – haemorrhagic stroke

Tangential speech: speech including additional information, irrelevant to the topic

Temporal lobe: the lower middle part of each side of the brain. Thought to be involved in memory function, among other things

Tracheostomy: a temporary surgical opening at the throat to assist breathing

Traumatic brain injury (TBI): an acquired brain injury caused by an external physical force, e.g. in an accident or as a non-accidental injury

Tremor: involuntary quivering movements

Unilateral: relating to only one side of the body

Unilateral neglect: lack of awareness either of one side of a person's own body, of anything external to one side of the body, or of both

Ventilator: a machine that maintains a flow of air into and out of the lungs when someone is unable to breathe normally

Ventricles: four cavities within the brain that are filled with cerebrospinal fluid

Index